falling clouberries

A WORLD
OF FAMILY RECIPES

MY MOTHER'S NAME IS SIRPA TUULA KERTTU PEIPONEN
MY FATHER'S NAME IS GEORGE

falling cloudberries

A WORLD
OF FAMILY RECIPES

Tessa Kiros

PHOTOGRAPHY BY MANOS CHATZIKONSTANTIS
STYLING BY MICHAIL TOUROS
ART DIRECTION BY LISA GREENBERG

MURDOCH BOOKS

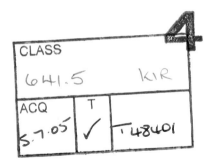
Published in 2004 by Murdoch Books Pty Limited

Murdoch Books Pty Limited Australia
Pier 8/9, 23 Hickson Road, Millers Point NSW 2000
Phone + 61 (0) 2 8220 2000 Fax + 61 (0) 2 8220 2558

Murdoch Books UK Limited
Erico House, 6th Floor North, 93/99 Upper Richmond Road, Putney, London SW15 2TG
Phone: + 44 (0) 20 8785 5995   Fax: + 44 (0) 20 8785 5985

Photography: Manos Chatzikonstantis
Food Styling and Illustrations: Michail Touros
Art Direction: Lisa Greenberg
Additional Design: Jacqueline Duncan and Tracy Loughlin
Cover Design: Marylouise Brammer

Editor: Jane Price
Food Editor: Katy Holder
Recipe Testing: Jo Glynn
Production: Monika Paratore
Editorial Director: Diana Hill

Chief Executive: Juliet Rogers
Publisher: Kay Scarlett

National Library of Australia Cataloguing-in-Publication Data: Kiros, Tessa. Falling cloudberries.
Includes index. ISBN 1 74045 364 6. I Cookery, International. II Title 641.59

Printed in China by 1010 Printing International Ltd. Reprinted in 2004,2005 (twice).

PAPPOU   ISO ISÄ

This book is dedicated to my grandfathers,
Pappou and Iso Isä. And to my parents,
George and Sipi, who inherited their special souls.
Thank goodness for everywhere you took us.

Contents

food from many kitchens

These are the recipes I grew up with: the recipes that have woven their way through the neighbourhoods of my mind, past indifference and into love. Those that have stayed while others might have fluttered away with a gentle spring breeze. These are the ones I choose to share; the ones that special people have taught me and that I have recorded, sometimes over a pot of coffee at my own kitchen table, and sometimes struggling to understand through the barriers of language on a journey somewhere.

I can remember the smell of those sweets my Cypriot grandmother gave us; their block shapes and bright wrappings, peppered with the eclecticism of South Africa, where we participated in Jewish Sabbath dinners at our friends' homes and sucked on butter-scotch bars at Scottish fetes on days off from our Greek school.

Both my wonderful grandfathers managed to fill me with a sense of appreciation for details. My Finnish Iso Isä would amaze us with Christmas parcels of enormous rye breads and Marimekko tablecloths, and the candles that would eventually grace the table for our Christmas Eve dinner. My Cypriot grandfather would arrive, carrying some pickled baby birds in a jar that would disgust us and have us yelping in conspiratorial glee. Who would have to sit next to the birds? Who would manage to hold in their laughter? We preferred him at his coals, turning the lamb or souvlaki, or standing in his back shed, frying chips and artichoke bottoms and knowing the exact moment to bash at them with his wooden spoon and make the crispy broken bits that we all fought over. At any given moment, he might calmly walk in and announce that the rice pudding was ready. Who wanted it with rose water; who preferred cinnamon?

At the same time I could imagine Iso Isä, stirring his Finnish mustard pot or poking out the freshest salmon at the fish market for gravadlax, arms full of dill and weaving his way home through all those strawberry tops left on the ground.

My mother taught us a few unnecessary phrases in Finnish, so that when I arrived I was able to say, "Grandfather, this is my hand," (of course, he wasn't at all surprised at this). We did feature in the local newspaper that week for my mother having moved away and come back after so long. There were all her friends from school, serving meatballs with lingonberry jam as though she had never been away. They grew up eating cloudberry puddings and things we had never even heard of in South Africa. I remember stories of falling cloudberries, summer houses on lakes and a lot of eucalyptus.

I love tradition, and gatherings of people around traditional events, and I have had a great mixture. Born in London to a Finnish mother and a Greek-Cypriot father, we moved to South Africa when I was four. I now live in Italy, and for some years here had a housekeeper from Peru. I have always kept my favourite recipes in journals and I hope you will find a place for them among your own tablecloths. Here are the recipes that I love.

family tree

KATERINA MENCHAKOV
great-great-grandmother
(russia)

*

SIRPA TUULA
KERTTU
PEIPONEN

mother
(finland)

SOJA
great-grandmother
(finland)

JOHANNES PEIPONEN
great-grandfather
(finland)

*

ISO ISÄ
VALTTER VLADIMIR PEIPONEN
grandfather
(finland)

TERTTU
SORANNE
grandmother
(finland)

*

*

VANIA
aunt

PAPPOU
PAPPOU KIROS
grandfather
(cyprus)

YAYIA OLGA PETSAS
grandmother
(cyprus)

GEORGE
father
(cyprus)

(LUD) TANJA
sister

NICHOLAS
brother

CASSIA

ME

GIOVANNI
husband
(italy)

YASMINE

FALLING
CLOUDBERRIES

'SIPI' AS A CHILD CARRYING *chamomile*

Finland

I remember opening the long-awaited Christmas parcels from our meticulous Finnish grandfather. We would be amazed at how perfectly they were always wrapped. Those beautiful candles, and the mantelipiparkakkuja (they were the biscuits). We would fall about doubled over with laughter as we tried to pronounce these names. Finland still remains a dream; a faraway land where Father Christmas lives and glides here and there with his sleigh, ducking through falling cloudberries and past my mother ice-skating to school.

MY ISO ISÄ
finland

SIRPA TUULA KERTTU PEIPONEN (sipi)
valkeakoski finland

Serves 4

4 LIGHTLY SMOKED SALTED HERRINGS
  (about 1 kg/2 lb 4 oz), *gutted*
500 ml (2 cups) LIGHT RED WINE VINEGAR
ABOUT 120 g (4½ oz) SUGAR
1 TEASPOON WHOLE PEPPERCORNS
1 FLAT TEASPOON WHOLE ALLSPICE (PIMENTO)
  BERRIES
3 BAY LEAVES
A SMALL HANDFUL OF DILL OR WILD FENNEL
  SPRIGS, *roughly chopped*
3 ONIONS, *cut into rings*
2 LARGISH CARROTS, *sliced*

HERRINGS MARINATED
IN VINEGAR WITH DILL
& ALLSPICE

This is how my mother makes her herrings. There are many ways to marinate and serve herrings and these are my favourite, marinated in vinegar, some sugar, carrots, onions, dill and allspice. I also like them done with tomato and onion. They need to stay in their marinade for about three days before you eat them. Keep the jar in the fridge and make sure that the herrings are immersed in the liquid. They will keep for about a week in the fridge and the flavour will get stronger. I use lightly smoked salted herrings and you can also use unsmoked if you prefer. You might also like to add a dried red chilli to your jar. These herrings are good served with room temperature potatoes that have been boiled with salt and dill stalks, or rye bread.

Rinse the herrings and soak them overnight in cold water, changing it a couple of times.

To fillet a herring, cut off the head and tail and then open the fish out flat, skin side up. Using your thumb, press down firmly along the backbone. This will nearly release the bones from the flesh. Turn the fish over and use scissors to snip through the backbone at the head and tail. Pull away the backbone, working towards the tail end. Remove any stray bones with your fingers or tweezers. Wash the fish and pat it dry. Cut the herring fillets into 2–3 cm (1 inch) strips.

Meanwhile, boil the vinegar, sugar, peppercorns and 250 ml (1 cup) water in a small pan for a few minutes, stirring to make sure the sugar has dissolved. Remove from the heat and add the allspice and bay leaves. Leave to cool down completely.

Layer the herring strips in jars with the dill, onion rings and carrots. Pour the cooled liquid into the jars, put on the lids tightly and keep refrigerated. Marinate for three days (or at least 24 hours if you're in a hurry) before serving. The herrings are also good drained of vinegar and served on a plate with a drizzle of olive oil.

Finland

Serves 4

1 SMALL RED ONION, *finely chopped*
1/2 TEASPOON SALT
2 LEMONS
2 HARD-BOILED EGGS
200 g (7 oz) SMOKED SALMON, *thinly sliced*
50 g (13/4 oz) DRAINED BABY CAPERS
15 g (1/4 cup) CHOPPED DILL
4 HEAPED TEASPOONS SALMON ROE

SMOKED
SALMON PLATE

This is an elegant yet simple way to serve smoked salmon (or gravadlax). You can add anything else you like — some cucumbers, sour cream or crème fraiche — depending on the ingredients you have at hand. Serve this with melba toast, potato pancakes or hapankorpuja, or other rye bread. Hard-boil the eggs for 7–8 minutes.

Put the onion in a small bowl, cover with water, sprinkle with the salt and leave to soak for 20 minutes or so. Rinse well, drain and pat dry with kitchen paper before putting back in the bowl.

To make lemon fillets, slice the tops and bottoms off the lemons. Sit the lemons on a board and, with a small sharp knife, cut downwards to remove the skin and pith. Holding the lemon over a bowl, remove the segments by slicing between the white pith. Remove any pips. Squeeze out any juice left in the lemon 'skeleton', then discard the skeleton.

Peel the eggs and separate the whites from the yolks. Finely chop each part and put into separate bowls.

To serve, arrange about four slices of salmon on each plate. Form small individual mounds of capers, dill, salmon roe, lemon fillets, chopped egg white, chopped egg yolk and onion around the salmon. Drizzle lemon juice over the salmon and season with ground black pepper before serving with your favourite bread.

Serves 15–20

300 g (10¹/₂ oz) CASTER (SUPERFINE) SUGAR
200 g (7 oz) COARSE SALT
150 g (5 oz) DILL, *chopped*
2 WHOLE FILLETS OF SALMON, *skin left on,*
  but cleaned and small bones removed

dill cucumbers
1 CUCUMBER
1 TABLESPOON CHOPPED DILL
100 ml (3¹/₂ fl oz) WHITE WINE VINEGAR
2 HEAPED TABLESPOONS CASTER
  (SUPERFINE) SUGAR
1 TEASPOON SALT

CHOPPED DILL, *to serve*
FINNISH MUSTARD (OPPOSITE), *to serve*

GRAVADLAX WITH DILL CUCUMBERS

Serve this with potato pancakes or rye bread, some home-made mustard and freshly chopped dill or dill crème fraîche.

To make the gravadlax, combine the sugar, salt, dill and a few good grindings of black pepper in a bowl. Put a large piece of foil on your work surface. Onto this put about a third of the sugar and salt mix. Put one salmon fillet, skin side down, on top of the mix then top this with another third of the mixture. Top with the other salmon fillet, skin side up, and cover with the remaining mixture. Pat down so it is all covered nicely and wrap the foil around to seal the salmon. Keep it in a container in the fridge for four days, turning it over every day. If you don't have a container large enough, sit it on a tray or large dish to catch any juices that may drip.

To make the dill cucumbers, cut the cucumber into very thin slices, slightly on the diagonal if you like, so that they are extra long and look good. Put them in a bowl where they will fit compactly in a few layers, sprinkling the dill between the layers. Combine the vinegar, sugar, salt and 2 tablespoons of water, stirring to dissolve the sugar and salt. Pour this over the cucumber to cover it. Keep in the fridge for at least a few hours before serving. Transfer to a jar and cover with its liquid and it will keep for up to a week.

To serve the gravadlax, remove the foil and scrape off as much of the sugar and salt mixture as possible. Slice the salmon very thinly, horizontally, and scatter with more fresh dill. Serve with the dill cucumbers and some Finnish mustard.

Makes 300 ml (10^1/$_2$ fl oz)

45 g (¹/₃ cup) HOT ENGLISH MUSTARD POWDER
115 g (¹/₂ cup) CASTER (SUPERFINE) SUGAR
1 TEASPOON SALT
250 ml (1 cup) POURING (SINGLE) CREAM
1 TABLESPOON OLIVE OIL
2 TABLESPOONS APPLE CIDER (OR OTHER)
  VINEGAR
JUICE OF HALF A LEMON

FINNISH
MUSTARD

We almost always had a jar of this in the house: my mother loves her mustard. This is wonderful — so quick to make and it will keep well for a few weeks in a glass jar in the fridge. You could find it becomes essential for cold meat sandwiches, roast ham and with smoked sausages and gravadlax. I imagine it would be nice with any mustard powder you use, but this is the way my mother always makes it.

Mix the mustard powder, sugar and salt together in a bowl, squashing out the lumps with a wooden spoon. Put in a small saucepan over low heat with the cream, oil, vinegar and lemon juice and bring to the boil, stirring constantly. Cook for 7–8 minutes, stirring often, then remove from the heat when it darkens and thickens. Stir now and then while it cools and then pour into glass jars. Store it in two shorter jars rather than a tall jar where it will be difficult to reach the last bit of mustard with a spoon. Keep in the fridge.

...there were always those stories of summer houses on lakes with eucalyptus, and hot-to-the-limit saunas...

Makes about 18

500 g (1 lb 2 oz) POTATOES, *peeled and halved*
125 ml (1/2 cup) POURING (SINGLE) CREAM
50 g (13/4 oz) PLAIN (ALL-PURPOSE) FLOUR,
  sifted
A LITTLE GRATED NUTMEG
3 EGGS, *separated*
BUTTER, *for shallow-frying*
OLIVE OIL, *for shallow-frying*

POTATO PANCAKES

These are wonderful with the richness of salmon and I like to serve them with the gravadlax and dill cucumbers. But they are also good with a fried egg, onions, bacon, sausages with mustard, or just warm spread with butter. You could add some freshly chopped herbs to the batter if you like. Keep them warm in a basket covered with a cloth until you are ready to serve.

Boil the potatoes for about 15 minutes in salted water until they are soft. Pass them through a food mill and then stir in the cream. Add the flour, nutmeg and some pepper and mix through well. Leave to cool a little.

Lightly whisk the egg yolks and whisk into the cooled potatoes. Whip the egg whites to soft peaks and fold those into the potato batter. Add a little more salt if necessary.

Melt a little butter and olive oil to cover the bottom of a frying pan over medium heat. When hot, drop in spoonfuls of the batter. Cook for 1–2 minutes until golden on the underside, then flip them swiftly over. Cook until golden, then lift out and keep warm. Add more butter and olive oil to the pan when necessary and cook the rest of the pancakes. Serve warm with salmon and a dollop of mustard.

Serves 6–8

1 kg (2 lb 4 oz) PIECE OF SALMON FILLET
ABOUT 8 WHOLE PEPPERCORNS
1 LONG STRIP OF LEMON RIND
1 LARGE CARROT, *cut into 3 chunks*
1 CELERY STALK TOP WITH LEAVES
3 BAY LEAVES
A FEW PARSLEY STALKS
A GOOD HANDFUL OF DILL
1 WHITE ONION
ABOUT 8 WHOLE ALLSPICE (PIMENTO) BERRIES
900 g (2 lb) POTATOES, *peeled and cut into large cubes*
200 ml (7 fl oz) POURING (SINGLE) CREAM
30 g (1 oz) BUTTER

FRESH SALMON,
DILL & POTATO
SOUP

This is a rich creamy soup, sufficient as a single course with a green side salad. It is very good served with slices of white bread that have been pan-fried in butter. You could also serve it with just-grilled bread. Get your fishmonger to give you the salmon central bone with tail if possible, so that you can make a good broth.

Skin the salmon and remove all the bones, feeling where they are by running your hand up and down the fish. Cut the salmon into chunks about 6 x 4 cm (2 inches square).

To make your broth, put about 3 litres (12 cups) of water into a large saucepan with a bit of the salmon skin, the salmon bones, peppercorns, lemon rind, carrot, celery, bay leaves, parsley stalks, some of the dill stalks, the whole onion and some salt. Bring to the boil and skim the surface of any scum. Lower the heat and simmer for about half an hour before straining into a large clean saucepan. You will need about 6 cupfuls: if you don't have enough, top up with some extra water.

Place the stock over high heat and add the allspice berries and potatoes. Simmer for about 15 minutes until the potatoes are just soft. Add the salmon chunks, lower the heat and simmer for about 10 minutes until the salmon is cooked. Add the cream, butter and the remaining chopped dill. Bring back to a gentle boil. Taste for salt and serve with a grinding of black pepper.

Serves 4 as a starter or snack

4 FRESH HERRINGS (about 1 kg/2 lb 4 oz), *gutted*
A PINCH OF WHITE PEPPER
20 g (1/3 cup) CHOPPED DILL
8 VERY THIN SLICES OF LEMON, *peel and pips removed*
1 EGG, *beaten*
125 g (1 cup) PLAIN (ALL-PURPOSE) FLOUR
ABOUT 50 g (2 oz) BUTTER
2 TABLESPOONS OLIVE OIL
LEMON WEDGES, *to serve*

FRIED STUFFED HERRINGS

This is my mother's friend Iria's recipe. She says this is autumn food in Finland, when the fishing boats anchor near the market places and you can buy really fresh herrings. These are also delicious sandwiched together with the dill and then barbecued in a fish rack over hot coals. Squeeze a lemon over them just before you serve. Whole herrings are also very good on the barbecue, just sprinkled with salt and pepper and then served with lemon juice and olive oil.

To fillet and clean a herring, cut off the head and tail, then open the fish out flat, skin side up. Using your thumb, press down firmly along the backbone. This will nearly release the bones from the flesh. Turn the fish over and use scissors to snip through the backbone at the head and tail. Pull away the backbone, working towards the tail end. Remove any stray small bones with your fingers or tweezers. Cut the fish into two fillets down the back. Wash the fish and pat dry.

Put one piece of fish, skin side down, on a wooden board. Sprinkle with salt and white pepper and put a heap of chopped dill on it. Add two of the thin lemon slices. Put another herring fillet on top of it, skin side up, as if you were making a sandwich. Repeat with the remaining fish.

Put the egg in a dish where you can comfortably turn the herring sandwiches around to coat them completely, then pat them gently with flour.

Heat the butter and oil in a non-stick frying pan. Fry the herrings, turning them over with a pair of tongs when you are sure the underneath is golden and firm. Sprinkle the done side with a little salt and pepper. Serve immediately with lemon wedges.

Serves 4–6

3 SLICES WHITE BREAD, *crusts removed*
160 ml (²/₃ cup) MILK
1 kg (2 lb 4 oz) MINCED (GROUND) PORK AND BEEF
1 LARGE EGG
1 RED ONION, *finely chopped*
2 TEASPOONS GROUND ALLSPICE (PIMENTO)
60 g (2¹/₄ oz) BUTTER
2 TABLESPOONS OLIVE OIL
1 TABLESPOON PLAIN (ALL-PURPOSE) FLOUR
200 g (7 oz) SOUR CREAM
LINGONBERRY OR CRANBERRY JAM (SEE OVER), *to serve*

FINNISH MEATBALLS WITH ALLSPICE, SOUR CREAM & LINGONBERRIES

This is so Finnish and probably one of the dishes that really remains in my mind from my childhood. Allspice is very popular in Finland; its taste is a combination of nutmeg, cinnamon, cloves and black pepper and it can be ground or in berry form. If you are not sure that what you have got in your spice rack is, in fact, allspice, then use less than indicated here and add a little more later (I once ended up with a very liquorice-tasting mince meat). You can use ordinary cream instead of the sour cream here. You can also use a bought jam if you can find one, but this jam is really so quick and simple to make.

Soak the bread in the milk in a large bowl for about 30 minutes or until it has absorbed all the milk and is very soft. Add the mince, egg, onion and allspice and season with salt and pepper. Knead together well with your hands, then form into small balls about the size of walnuts, rolling them between your palms so that they are compact and won't fall apart when cooking.

Heat 40 g (1¹/₂ oz) of the butter with the olive oil in a non-stick frying pan. Fry the meatballs in batches, turning them once during cooking. (You will have to work quite quickly and take care not to burn the butter and oil. If necessary, wipe out the pan between batches and start again with a little less butter and oil.) Transfer the cooked meatballs to a heavy-based saucepan with any onion that is on the bottom of the pan and continue with the next batch.

Sprinkle the flour into the frying pan and mix with a wooden spoon until it is smooth. Add the remaining butter and let it melt. Continue cooking, stirring almost continuously, until it is a golden colour. Remove the pan from the heat and very slowly pour in 500 ml (2 cups) hot water, standing back a bit. Mix in quickly, then return the pan to the heat. Stir in the sour cream and mix well, then carefully pour over the meatballs. Season lightly with salt and pepper and cook, covered, over very low heat for 10–15 minutes, until you have a thick creamy sauce with soft meatballs to serve with berry jam and boiled potatoes.

Makes about 500 ml (2 cups)

500 g (1 lb 2 oz) FROZEN *or* FRESH
   LINGONBERRIES *or* CRANBERRIES
200 g (7 oz) CASTER (SUPERFINE) SUGAR
FINELY GRATED RIND AND JUICE OF 1 LEMON
1 SMALL APPLE, *peeled and cored*

LINGONBERRY
OR CRANBERRY JAM

Lingonberries are everywhere in Finland, growing in clumps on small bushes. They make a tart, sourish jam that is delicious served with meats and game; try it with your Christmas turkey or alongside a baked ham. Make it in a heavy-based saucepan suitable for making jam. You might need to adjust the amount of sugar, depending on the tartness of your berries. The jam will be ready to eat once it has cooled, but you can also seal it in jars (while still hot) and store for when you need it.

Rinse the berries, if necessary, then drain well and put them in a non-metallic bowl with the sugar and lemon juice. Leave overnight, turning once or twice.

Coarsely grate the apple and put it into a jam-making pan or other heavy-based saucepan with the grated lemon rind. Strain in all the juice from the berries and add two wooden-spoonfuls of berries, leaving the rest of the berries in the bowl for now. Add 125 ml (1/2 cup) water and simmer for 20–30 minutes, or until the apple is very soft and the whole lot has thickened. Add the rest of the berries and heat through for 5–8 minutes. Pour into sterilised jars. Seal tightly and turn upside down. Cover with a cloth and leave to cool completely, before turning upright and storing in a cool place. The jam will keep for a couple of months but, once open, keep it in the fridge and use fairly quickly.

Ritva's Finnish dinner

Some afternoons in South Africa my mother would invite her Irish, Scottish and Finnish friends around and we would eat the cakes that everyone had baked and play with their children.

When her Finnish friend, Ritva, came round, I would listen to them clucking away loudly in their native tongue. I could recognise the numbers (my mother still always counts in Finnish). I collected many recipes from Ritva and one special night we organised a Finnish dinner. It began with the caviar that a friend had flown in for her. Then we had a smoked salmon platter with various garnishes, and followed with her stroganoff of beef and pickled cucumbers, with lots of boiled potatoes and parsley. Later we ate cinnamon and cardamom buns, slightly warm, with some crème anglaise for dipping into. Ritva had thought to bring Finnish cassettes with her and all the while they were playing in the background.

I am crazy about evenings like this.

Serves 4–6

1.5 kg (3 lb 5 oz) PIECE OF LEAN SILVERSIDE
  or TOPSIDE OF BEEF
2 LARGE CARROTS, *cut into chunks*
1 LARGE RED ONION, *cut into quarters*
ABOUT 8 ALLSPICE (PIMENTO) BERRIES
1 BAY LEAF
125 ml (¹/₂ cup) POURING (SINGLE) CREAM
2 TABLESPOONS CHOPPED PARSLEY

BEEF CASSEROLE
WITH CARROTS, ONIONS
& CREAM

This is adapted from a popular Finnish dish called Karelian stew, which uses a few different types of meat in the same pot, giving it a special flavour. It is a very simply cooked dish — rustic and wintery and quite undemanding. You could add a few fresh herbs or other spices if you like, or even try a variety of meats (veal, beef and pork). This has a long, slow cooking time and is sometimes even left in the oven overnight.

Preheat your oven to 180°C (350°F/Gas 4). Put all the ingredients except the cream and parsley into a heavy casserole and add about 750 ml (3 cups) water, or enough to come about three-quarters of the way up the side of the meat.

Cover the casserole and bake for about 2 hours, turning the meat over a couple of times until it is really soft. Remove from the oven. Lift out the carrots and onion with a slotted spoon and pass them through the fine disc of a food mill, or purée them. Discard the bay leaf and allspice berries from the casserole. Remove the meat from the casserole and keep warm.

Measure about 750 ml (3 cups) of the cooking liquid and return this with the puréed vegetables to the casserole (you can freeze the leftover cooking broth for another use). Add the cream and the parsley and heat through. Adjust the seasoning if necessary. Serve the meat thickly sliced with a lot of sauce poured over it.

Serves 4

pastry
225 g (8 oz) PLAIN (ALL-PURPOSE) FLOUR
225 g (8 oz) CHILLED BUTTER, *diced*
4–5 TABLESPOONS ICED WATER

40 g (1½ oz) BUTTER
2 TABLESPOONS OLIVE OIL
600 g (1 lb 5 oz) PIECE OF PORK FILLET
4 GARLIC CLOVES
2 *or* 3 SAGE SPRIGS
60 ml (¼ cup) BRANDY
300 g (10½ oz) MIXED WILD MUSHROOMS
125 ml (½ cup) POURING (SINGLE) CREAM

PORK FILLET IN PASTRY
WITH WILD MUSHROOMS
& CREAM SAUCE

This is lovely: a whole pork fillet, cooked with mushrooms and wrapped in a jacket of pastry. If you can't get fresh wild mushrooms, buy 10 g (¼ oz) dried wild mushrooms and soak them in a little water until they've plumped up. Make up the rest of the weight with ordinary mushrooms.

To make the pastry, sift the flour and a pinch of salt into a bowl. Add the butter and stir through to coat it with flour. Add enough of the iced water to make the dough come together. Gather into a ball and transfer to a floured work surface. Flour your hands and form the dough into a rectangular block. Roll this out to make a rectangle that is about 1 cm (½ inch) thick and has the short side closest to you. Fold up the bottom third of the rectangle and fold down the top third. Seal the edges lightly with a rolling pin. Turn the dough through 90 degrees and roll it out again into a rectangle that is about 5 mm (¼ inch) thick. Fold as before, turn the dough and roll out again. Do this once more, then put the dough in a plastic bag and leave in the fridge for 30 minutes. It can be frozen at this point if you won't be using it immediately, or the pastry can be kept in the fridge for a couple of days.

Meanwhile, preheat your oven to 200°C (400°F/Gas 6). Melt the butter with the oil in a casserole dish on the stovetop. Brown the pork quite quickly, seasoning the browned sides with salt and pepper. Add the garlic and sage and cook for a few seconds before adding the brandy. Either ignite the brandy and let it burn out, or just let it evaporate. Add the mushrooms around the meat, seasoning them with a little salt and pepper.

Put the dish in the oven and cook for 20 minutes, turning the pork over once or twice and shuffling the mushrooms. The pork should be nicely browned and cooked through, but still slightly pink inside (it will get more time in the oven in the pastry jacket). Remove the pork to a plate to cool and leave the mushrooms with any juice in the dish.

Take your pastry out of the fridge and flatten it out on a lightly floured surface to make a rectangle that is about 30 x 25 cm (12 x 10 inches). Lay the pork fillet along one long side, towards the bottom, and roll up the pastry around it. Pinch the ends together and fold them up over the top of the fillet. Put on a baking tray lined with baking paper, reduce the oven to 180°C (350°F/Gas 4) and cook for about 30 minutes, or until the pastry is nicely golden and cooked through and the bottom is also golden and firm. Remove from the oven and leave to stand while you finish the sauce.

Put the casserole dish with the mushrooms on the stovetop and add about 125 ml (½ cup) water, scraping up any bits from the bottom. Bring to the boil, let it thicken slightly and then add the cream. As soon as it comes to a rolling simmer, remove from the heat and season. If the sauce seems too thin, leave it to simmer for a little longer.

Slice the pork and serve immediately with a little of the sauce spooned on the side. Don't spoon sauce all over the pastry or it will become soggy.

My mother always talks of how they collected wild mushrooms in the woods in thin wooden plaited baskets. The pines and birches and other trees were at their most splendid and the mushrooms were fantastic that same night, sautéed in butter with onions.

Serves 3

2 EGGS
1 GARLIC CLOVE, *finely chopped*
$^1/_2$ TEASPOON SWEET PAPRIKA
1 TEASPOON FINELY CHOPPED ROSEMARY LEAVES
6 x 60 g (2$^1/_4$ oz) SLICES PORK LOIN (about 1 cm/$^1/_2$ inch thick)
50 g ($^2/_3$ cup) FRESH BREADCRUMBS
BUTTER, *for frying*
LEMON WEDGES, *to serve*

PORK SCHNITZELS

This easy dish can be made at the last moment or way beforehand. Schnitzels are great for a picnic or in sandwiches and are quite adaptable to any 'smorgasbord'. You could add a little ginger and soy to the marinade for an oriental touch, or leave out all the garlic and herbs and make it completely plain, using any type of meat — chicken, lamb chops, veal, beef or turkey. Serve plain, with lemon, or with a special mayonnaise such as balsamic or lemon tarragon. We always made an enormous pile of these in our house as they are great eaten cold the next day. The pile would get smaller and smaller until eventually just the empty plate sat alone in the fridge and my mother would be left serving salad, sautéed potatoes and bread for next day's lunch.

Whisk the eggs in a large bowl. Season with salt and pepper, then whisk in the garlic, paprika and rosemary. Put the slices of pork in the egg mix, turning them over to make sure they are all well coated. Leave to marinate for at least 15 minutes.

Put the breadcrumbs on a plate. Take the meat out of the marinade, letting the excess drip off, and then pat into the breadcrumbs on both sides, pressing down with the heel of your palm to make sure that the breadcrumbs stick.

Heat enough butter in a saucepan to shallow-fry the meat. Add the pork and fry quickly, turning so that both sides are nicely golden brown and the meat is cooked through. You could add a little olive oil if you are nervous about the butter burning, but it shouldn't be a problem. If your pan is not big enough to accommodate all the slices, cook them in two lots, but you may have to wipe out the pan between batches. Serve hot, at room temperature or cold, with a squeeze of lemon juice and a little extra salt if necessary.

Serves 3 as a side dish

800 g (1 lb 12 oz) POTATOES, *peeled and cut into 3 cm*
   (1¹/₄ inch) *chunks*
2 TABLESPOONS OLIVE OIL
1 RED ONION, *chopped*
30 g (1 oz) BUTTER
2 GARLIC CLOVES, *lightly crushed with the flat of a knife*
1 TEASPOON CHOPPED THYME LEAVES
1 FRESH BAY LEAF
2 TABLESPOONS CHOPPED PARSLEY

SAUTEED
POTATOES

These are nice with sausages and mustard, schnitzels, pork chops... just about any meat.

Boil the potatoes in salted water for 10 minutes or so, until they are cooked through but not too soft. Drain well.

Heat half the oil in a non-stick pan. Add the onion and sauté gently for about 15 minutes, until it is softened and beginning to look a bit sticky in the pan. Remove to a plate and wipe out the pan if necessary.

Add the butter and remaining oil to the pan. Add the potatoes, garlic and thyme and sauté over medium heat. Once the bottoms of the potatoes begin to brown, lower the heat slightly and leave them to get crusty and golden, tossing carefully from time to time. Take care not to break them up too much and try to keep them more or less in one flat layer. If the garlic looks like it is browning too much, sit it on top of the potatoes. After nearly 20 minutes add the bay leaf and continue to sauté.

When the potatoes are quite golden and crisp in parts (like a cross between soft-boiled potatoes and chips), toss the onion and parsley through, cook for another minute or so and then remove from the heat. Season with salt and pepper before serving.

Serves 16

1 x 6 kg (13 lb) HAM
80 g (1 cup) FRESH BREADCRUMBS
95 g (½ cup) BROWN SUGAR
1 QUANTITY FINNISH MUSTARD (PAGE 27)
12–15 WHOLE CLOVES

BAKED
HAM

This is a classic in my family. We always had this for our 'Scandinavian' Christmas Eve dinner, when the ham was often decorated with red and white ribbons tied around the bone. It is wonderful for the days that follow as well, as it is so big and people can just slice bits off whenever they feel like it. Often a pea soup is made with the leftover bone. It is easy to find a ready-salted ham in most parts of the world, although in Italy I cannot, so I often prepare it myself. Because I don't use saltpetre for the preserving, my ham is not as pink as those you will buy. If you are going to cure your ham yourself, you should be extra careful with the brining process, especially if you won't be using a preserving agent. I buy a leg of pork of about 6–7 kg (15 lb) and I mix 4 tablespoons of salt and 2 tablespoons of sugar and rub it over the cleaned and skinned pork, then leave it for a day in a cool place. Next I boil up a brine for a few minutes, using 800 g (1 lb 12 oz) salt, 10 litres of water, 10 peppercorns and a few bay leaves. When this has cooled completely, I sink the pork leg in, making sure it is completely covered in liquid, and leave it for about 8 days, turning it over from time to time. Then I rinse it with cold water, pat it dry, sprinkle it with salt and pepper and wrap it in foil. I bake it at 220°C (425°F/ Gas 7) for 30 minutes, then turn the oven down to 180°C (350°F/Gas 4) and bake it for another 3½ hours. I turn it from time to time, until the ham is cooked through and hardly any liquid oozes out if I poke it with a skewer. Let it cool for a bit, before glazing it as follows.

Put the ham on an oven rack that will fit over an oven dish. Mix together the breadcrumbs and brown sugar. Paint the mustard all over the ham, reaching as far underneath as you can. It might be easier to work with your hands as the mustard will start melting. Sprinkle the breadcrumb and sugar mixture all over the ham, throwing handfuls at the side to make it stick. Spike cloves in the top of the ham to make a rough diamond pattern. Only the very underneath of your ham should be bare.

Bake the ham for 45 minutes–1 hour, or until the top is golden and crusty, turning the oven up a bit for the end of the cooking if necessary. Leave the ham to cool before slicing. Serve with Finnish mustard and lingonberry jam.

Syksyn
Koriste-
kurpitsat

1,5€

KATERINA MENCHAKOV
(my great-great-grandmother)
russia

Serves 6 as a side dish

1.3 kg (3 lb) POTATOES
3 RED ONIONS, *chopped*
750 ml (3 cups) POURING (single) CREAM

OVEN-COOKED
POTATOES WITH ONIONS
& CREAM

This is definitely my mother's special dish: I always remember her making it to go with the baked ham for Christmas. Serve these deliciously soft and very creamy potatoes with a simple roast meat, slices of baked ham or a roast chicken. They are more attractive as a partner to simply cooked meats and might be too heavy with a rich dish, although this depends on your own taste. You could easily add fresh chopped herbs to the potatoes before cooking.

Preheat your oven to 190°C (375°F/Gas 5). Cut the potatoes into small chips, about 5 x 0.5 cm (2 x ¼ inch). Put them in a shallow oven dish, add the onions and season well with salt and pepper. Mix together thoroughly with your hands. Drizzle the cream over the top, making sure it covers all the potato. Cover the dish with aluminium foil and bake for about 1½ hours. Remove the foil and bake for another 30 minutes, or until the potatoes and onions are really soft and have absorbed most of the cream. There should still be a little thickened liquid in the pan. Serve not too hot.

Serves 6 as a side dish

6 FAIRLY LARGE POTATOES
50 g (1³/4 oz) BUTTER
2 TABLESPOONS OLIVE OIL
A HANDFUL OF SAGE LEAVES

HASSELBACK
POTATOES

Hasselbacks are gorgeous: they have style and show up a beautiful crust and texture. They look a bit like Persian shutters. Try adding a couple of tablespoons of pesto (page 306) to the cooked potatoes, spooning the pan juices over as well so that they are nicely oiled and the pesto runs into the cavities. Roast them for another 5 or 10 minutes and serve immediately. A nice, not-too-hot, grainy mustard works well, too. Choose rounded potatoes that will sit nicely on the tray once they have been halved and still have a good bulge of volume to sculpt.

Preheat your oven to 220°C (425°F/Gas 7). Peel the potatoes and cut them in half lengthways. Sit them, flat side down, on a chopping board. Using a small sharp knife, start at one end of the potato and cut down through the top, about a third of the way through. Make another cut about 1 mm away from the first, slightly on the diagonal towards the first cut, and break away the little piece of potato to make a slit. Continue along the potato, making slits about 5 mm (¹/4 inch) apart.

Handling the potatoes carefully so that they don't break, arrange them in a baking dish. Add the butter and oil and season with salt and pepper. Scatter the sage leaves around and bake for 45 minutes – 1 hour, or until the potatoes are golden and crispy. Spoon a little of the buttery pan juices over the top from time to time and gently shuffle them so they don't stick (but don't touch them for the first 15 minutes or so or they will simply break.) Serve immediately.

Finland

Serves 8–10

220 g (1¾ cups) CAKE FLOUR OR PLAIN
  (ALL-PURPOSE) FLOUR, *plus extra for dusting*
180 g (¾ cup) SUGAR
3 TEASPOONS BAKING POWDER
180 g (6 oz) BUTTER, *melted*
185 ml (¾ cup) WARM MILK
4 EGGS, *separated*
1 TEASPOON VANILLA EXTRACT
800 g (1 lb 12 oz) STRAWBERRIES
1 TEASPOON LEMON JUICE
4 TABLESPOONS ICING (CONFECTIONERS') SUGAR
750 ml (3 cups) THICK (DOUBLE/HEAVY) CREAM

SIPI'S STRAWBERRY CAKE

The Finns are crazy about strawberries and my mother's kitchen is always full of them. This is the cake my mother still makes for a celebration. It is so lovely; really pure and pretty, just like the Finns.

Preheat the oven to 180°C (350°F/Gas 4). Grease and flour a 22 cm (8½ inch) springform cake tin, or a bundt pan.

Put the flour and sugar in a bowl with 1 teaspoon of the baking powder. Mix in the butter and then stir in the milk. Add the egg yolks and vanilla and beat in well. Whisk the egg whites to soft peaks, incorporating the rest of the baking powder when the eggs have started fluffing up. Fold the whites into the cake mixture.

Pour the batter into the cake tin and bake for about 1 hour or until a skewer inserted into the centre comes out clean and the top is deep golden and crisp. Remove from the oven and leave to cool a bit before turning out onto a rack. When cool, slice the cake in half horizontally and put the bottom half on a large serving plate.

Clean the strawberries and hull them (leave a few unhulled, if you prefer to see them that way on top of the cake). Dice about half the strawberries and sprinkle with a little lemon juice and 1 tablespoon of the icing sugar. Whip the cream into stiff peaks with the remaining icing sugar. Mix the diced strawberries with about a third of the whipped cream and spoon over the bottom of the cake. Put the other half of the cake on top and thickly spoon the remaining cream over the top and side, then decorate with the rest of the strawberries. This is best eaten immediately. Any leftovers will keep for a day in the fridge.

Makes about 35 buns

bun dough
250 ml (1 cup) TEPID MILK
100 g (3½ oz) CASTER (SUPERFINE) SUGAR
25 g (1 oz) FRESH YEAST
1 EGG, *lightly beaten*
125 g (4½ oz) BUTTER, *softened*
2 TEASPOONS GROUND CARDAMOM
1 TEASPOON SALT
650 g (5¼ cups) CAKE FLOUR OR PLAIN
  (ALL-PURPOSE) FLOUR

cinnamon butter
2 TEASPOONS GROUND CINNAMON
50 g (1¾ oz) CASTER (SUPERFINE) SUGAR,
  PLUS 1 TABLESPOON *for sprinkling*
80 g (2¾ oz) BUTTER, *softened*
1 EGG, *lightly beaten*

CINNAMON &
CARDAMOM BUNS

These gorgeous buns were always a part of my childhood. They are found everywhere in Finland — and probably all over Scandinavia — in tea rooms and houses. Everyone makes their own and they freeze beautifully so you can just pull out a few when a craving sets in. Don't be put off when you see that the buns need to rise for a couple of hours. You can get the dough together really quickly and then leave it alone without even a glance. The rolling and cutting can be a little tricky the first time you do it, but the second time will be easy.

Put the milk and sugar in a bowl and crumble in the yeast. Leave for 10 minutes, or until the yeast begins to activate. Add the egg, butter, cardamom and salt and mix in. Add the flour, bit by bit, mixing it in with a wooden spoon until you need to use your hands, and then turn it out onto the work surface to knead. It may seem a little too sticky initially, but will become compact and beautifully soft after about 5 minutes. Put the dough back in the bowl, cover with a clean cloth and then a heavy towel or blanket, and leave in a warm place for about 2 hours, or until it has doubled in size.

To make the cinnamon butter, mix together the cinnamon and sugar. Divide the butter into four portions and keep on one side.

Put the dough on a floured work surface and divide it into four portions. Begin with one portion, covering the others with a cloth so they don't dry out. Using a rolling pin, roll out a rectangle, roughly about 30 x 25 cm (12 x 10 inches) and 2–3 mm (1/8 inch) thick. Spread one portion of butter over the surface of the dough with a palette knife or blunt knife. Sprinkle with about 3 teaspoons of the cinnamon mix, covering the whole surface with quick shaking movements of your wrists. Roll up to make a long dough sausage. Set aside while you finish rolling out and buttering the rest of the dough, so that you can cut them all together.

Line two large baking trays with baking paper, or bake in two lots if you only have one tray. Line up the dough sausages in front of you and cut them slightly on the diagonal, alternating up and down, so that the slices are fat 'v' shapes, with the point of the 'v' about 2 cm (3/4 inch) and the base about 5 cm (2 inches). Turn them so they are all the right way up, sitting on their fatter bases. Press down on the top of each one with two fingers until you think you will almost go through to your work surface. Along the sides you will see the cinnamon stripes oozing outwards. Put the buns on the baking tray, leaving space for them to puff and rise while they bake. Brush lightly with beaten egg and sprinkle a little sugar over the top.

Leave the buns to rise for half an hour and preheat your oven to 180°C (350°F/Gas 4). Bake them for about 20 minutes, or until they are golden. Check that they are lightly golden underneath as well before you take them out of the oven. Serve hot, warm or at room temperature and, when they are cool, keep them in an airtight container so they don't harden.

Sini's fishing trips

My mother used to go fishing on the lakes with a rod and come home, glowing, carrying an aluminium bucket full of long bream. The fishermen had been busy with their nets and the market would later be spilling over with wooden boxes of herrings — all stacked on top of each other and shining in their silver jackets.

SIRPA TUULA KERTTI

Serves 6–8

500 g (1 lb 2 oz) FRESH *or* FROZEN CRANBERRIES
 or SIMILAR BERRIES
345 g (1¹/₂ cups) CASTER (SUPERFINE) SUGAR

CRANBERRY
SORBET

This is stunning: refreshing, slightly tart and such an inspiring colour to bring out of your kitchen. Sometimes I like to serve it with a shot of vodka or a gentle blob of whipped cream alongside. You could also add a little liqueur to the sorbet if you like. Unfortunately, this doesn't work too well without an ice-cream machine — you can beat it by hand, but you will end up with a sort of granita instead of a sorbet.

Wash the berries. Put in a pan with the sugar and 825 ml (3¹/₂ cups) water. Cover the pan and cook, stirring occasionally, for 10 minutes or so until the berries are soft. Purée, strain and leave to cool before freezing in your ice-cream machine according to the manufacturer's instructions.

The berries were always collected in the summer, some one by one and others in clumps. Baskets hung over one arm, they set off. There were so many wild berries — strawberries, blueberries, blackberries, cloudberries, greenberries, raspberries, gooseberries... just berries, berries everywhere. They would eat them plain at first. Then, later, press them into juice or stir them until they turned into jams.

OREGANO, ORANGES + OLIVE GROVES

Greece

OREGANO, ORANGES + OLIVE GROVES

I love the orange trees lining winter Athenian avenues. And the people who open their doors and their hearts to you. I love the Greek markets with baskets of gorgeous red just-flowered pistachios, piles of figs and very wild hilltop greens sitting next to indifferent mountains of underwear. Everywhere, amongst the pervasive smell of fresh oregano, there is an atmosphere of people doing their own thing, each stepping in tune to their own internal guide. Greece is magnetic, they say. Once you have stepped on Greek ground it's hard to shake yourself free. Myth has it that it's because your feet become stuck in the rich honey coating this country. It's the only place where people have always wished me a good week, month, day, summer, winter, life, work... and a birthday wish to grow old with white hair.

Makes about 26

5 TABLESPOONS OLIVE OIL
550 g (1 lb 4 oz) MINCED (GROUND) PORK AND BEEF
3 SPRING ONIONS (SCALLIONS), *finely chopped*
3 RIPE TOMATOES, *grated or peeled and puréed*
3 TABLESPOONS ROUGHLY CHOPPED PARSLEY
1 TEASPOON DRIED MINT, *crumbled*
1/2 TEASPOON GROUND CINNAMON
100 g (1/2 cup) UNCOOKED LONG-GRAIN RICE
230 g (8 oz) VINE LEAVES (450 g/1 lb *if bought in brine*)
40 g (1 1/2 oz) BUTTER
JUICE OF 1 LEMON, *plus extra, to serve*
PLAIN GREEK YOGHURT, *to serve*

DOLMADES
(STUFFED VINE LEAVES)

You can use fresh vine leaves or those bought in brine, but if you use frozen you'll need to blanch them in boiling water first. Also, you can try adding pine nuts, sultanas or other fresh herbs to the filling.

To make the filling, heat 3 tablespoons of the olive oil in a non-stick saucepan. Add the mince and sauté until it is just cooked and has begun to turn golden in places. Add the spring onions and sauté for a couple of minutes to soften. Season with salt and pepper. Add the tomatoes, parsley, mint, cinnamon and rice and mix through very well, cooking for an extra minute or so to slightly soften the rice. Remove from the heat and leave to cool slightly.

Prepare the vine leaves. Layer five or six imperfect leaves on the bottom of a large saucepan to prevent the dolmades sticking. Take another leaf and, holding it in your palm (shiny side down), put a tablespoon or so of filling neatly in the middle. (If your leaves are small you can use two together, slightly overlapping them.) To wrap up the leaves snugly, fold up the bottom part, then fold one side tightly over the stuffing, fold down the top part and then fold the other side around. Then roll it up to make a compact bundle. (You can make the dolmades as small as you like, just take care not to stretch the leaves too much or they may tear.) Layer the dolmades over the vine leaves lining the pan, making two or three layers if necessary. Dot with the butter and add about 750 ml (3 cups) of water. Drizzle the lemon juice and remaining olive oil over the top and season with a little salt.

Turn a plate over and put it on top of the dolmades so that it fits tightly in the saucepan and will hold them in shape while cooking. Bring to the boil, then lower the heat and simmer for about 1 hour, or until the dolmades are soft and juicy. There should still be some liquid in the bottom of the pan; if not, add a bit more water towards the end. Serve the dolmades hot or cold with lemon juice and a dollop of yoghurt.

Serves 6–8

2 GARLIC CLOVES, *very finely minced*
2 TABLESPOONS OLIVE OIL
1 TABLESPOON LEMON JUICE
1 SMALL CUCUMBER
1 TEASPOON SALT
600 g (1 lb 5 oz) THICK PLAIN GREEK
    YOGHURT
2 TEASPOONS DRIED MINT

TZATZIKI
(YOGHURT, CUCUMBER,
GARLIC & MINT DIP)

Use as much garlic as you like: this recipe has only two cloves. You could also soak the garlic in olive oil and then just strain the oil into the dip if you are against too much garlic. This is wonderful with grilled lamb, souvlakia, souvla or sheftalia; and it does well on a mixed meze platter with little meatballs and pitta bread for dipping. It is very versatile and you could make other variations to suit whatever you're serving. For grilled salmon or tuna you could add freshly chopped coriander (cilantro) or dill to the yoghurt.

Put the garlic, olive oil and lemon juice in a small bowl and leave on one side.

Peel the skin off the cucumber lengthways in alternate stripes — miss one, do one. Grate the cucumber coarsely and put it in a fine sieve in the sink. Sprinkle with the salt and leave for about half an hour to let the juices drip away. Squash it with your hands or a wooden spoon to extract the liquid (this will prevent your tzatziki being watery).

Put the yoghurt in a bowl and stir in the mint, crushing it between your fingers as you add it. Add the garlic oil mixture and cucumber and season with some black pepper. Mix through well, and taste for salt before serving.

If you aren't serving it immediately, store in a covered container in the fridge, where the flavours will mature. It should keep for a couple of days.

Serves 8–10

2 SLICES BREAD, *crusts removed*
1/2 RED ONION
125 g (41/2 oz) PURE TARAMA (or smoked cod's roe)
325 ml (11 fl oz) LIGHT OLIVE OIL
JUICE OF 2 LEMONS

TARAMASALATA

This is a well-known Greek dip traditionally made from smoked grey mullet roe, but you can also use smoked cod's roe. I like it a pale creamy salmon-beige colour, although it is often available in a brighter pink. The actual roe, which you may have to order from your fishmonger, is a burgundy-maroon colour and is strong and impossible to eat on its own. Taramasalata is served with bread or pitta, and also goes nicely on a meze with some raw vegetables for dipping. You could serve it alongside other fish meze, like a small plate of grilled octopus or some deep-fried calamari.

Soak the bread in a little water until it is soggy and then firmly squeeze out all of the water. Finely grate the onion and then squeeze the juice into a bowl (discard the onion pulp).

Put the tarama in a mixing bowl with the bread. Whisk together briefly with an electric whisk. Gradually add the olive oil slowly, whisking continuously. If it looks like curdling at any stage, add some of the lemon juice and whisk again until all of your olive oil is used up. Beat in the lemon and onion juices. You should have a lumpy-looking mayonnaise. Transfer to a blender and purée until just smooth, being careful not to overmix. This step may not be necessary if you achieve a smooth purée with the electric whisk. Transfer the taramasalata to a serving bowl. It will keep well, covered in the fridge, for a couple of days.

Serves 6 as a side dish

250 g (9 oz) DRIED CHICKPEAS (*without skins if possible*),
   soaked overnight in cold water, or 400 g (14 oz) TINNED
   CHICKPEAS
250 ml (1 cup) OLIVE OIL
1 LARGE RED ONION, *chopped*
5 GARLIC CLOVES, *very finely chopped*
1 *or* 2 RED CHILLIES, *seeded and finely chopped*
250 g (1²/₃ cups) CRUMBLED FETA CHEESE
4 SPRING ONIONS (SCALLIONS), GREEN PART ONLY,
   chopped
25 g (¹/₂ cup) CHOPPED CORIANDER (CILANTRO)
30 g (1 cup) CHOPPED FLAT-LEAF (ITALIAN) PARSLEY
JUICE OF 1 LEMON

CHICKPEA,
FETA & CORIANDER
SALAD

This is my friend Stephen's way of serving chickpeas. It can be made beforehand and left to marinate for a couple of hours before being served at room temperature. Make sure that everything has cooled before you mix it all together, or else the feta will melt. I bought skinned chickpeas in Greece, which worked well and, if you need to be a little more spontaneous, you can use tinned chickpeas. Serve with chicken breasts or lamb chops that have been marinated in cumin and yoghurt and then grilled.

If you're using tinned chickpeas, just rinse them and put them in a bowl. Otherwise, rinse the soaked chickpeas, put them in a saucepan, cover generously with water and bring to the boil. Lower the heat slightly and cook for 1–1¹/₂ hours, until they are soft but not falling apart, adding salt towards the end of the cooking time. Leave them in their liquid if you will not be making the salad right away. When cooled, drain and put the chickpeas in a large bowl, picking out as many of the loose skins as you can. (You can put them in a colander and shake roughly or rub them around with your hands, then pick out the skins.)

Heat 3 tablespoons of the olive oil and fry the red onion gently until it is cooked through and lightly golden. Add the garlic and chilli and cook for a few more seconds until you can smell the garlic. Take care not to brown the garlic. Leave to cool completely.

Add the feta, spring onion, coriander, parsley and lemon juice to the chickpeas and season with pepper and a dash more salt, if needed. Add the cooled garlic oil and the remaining olive oil and mix through very well.

Serves 4

1 CHICKEN (about 1.3 kg/3 lb)
1 WHITE ONION
1 CELERY STALK WITH LEAVES, *cut into large chunks*
1 LARGE CARROT, *cut into half*
A FEW PARSLEY STALKS
A FEW BLACK PEPPERCORNS
100 g (¹/₂ cup) LONG-GRAIN RICE, *rinsed*
2 EGGS
JUICE OF 2 LEMONS

AVGOLEMONO (CHICKEN SOUP WITH EGG & LEMON)

You could easily add some unauthentic thyme sprigs or other herbs to infuse the broth of this classic Greek soup. My aunt even makes avgolemono with lamb instead of chicken, to celebrate the end of the fast for Easter. It is rich and delicious, simple and nourishing, and gives you two courses from one recipe (the soup and then the beautiful poached chicken). Egg and lemon is very popular as a finish for soups and sauces in Greek cooking.

Rinse the chicken well and put it in a large stockpot with the onion, celery, carrot, parsley stalks, peppercorns and a good sprinkling of salt. Cover with about 3.5 litres (14 cups) of cold water and bring to the boil. Skim the surface with a slotted spoon, lower the heat and simmer, uncovered, for about 1¹/₂ hours, skimming occasionally. Lift the chicken out onto a plate with a slotted spoon. Strain the broth through a sieve, pressing down lightly on the vegetables with your wooden spoon to extract the flavour. You should have about 1.5 litres (6 cups) of broth. Return this to the saucepan, add the rice and cook over medium heat for another 15 minutes or so, until the rice is cooked.

Whisk the eggs until they are fluffy. Add the lemon juice. Add a ladleful of hot broth to the egg, whisking to stop it scrambling. Whisk in a little more broth, then add the whole lot to the pan. Return the saucepan to the lowest possible heat for a few minutes to warm the egg through. Add some salt and pepper and serve immediately. If you like, shred one of the chicken breasts and scatter over the soup. Serve the rest of the chicken as a second course.

I always long for those lunches that begin anywhere between noon and 5 pm and end only when the owner decides it's time to drag the tables off the beach and back across the road. We linger now, on the sand, finishing off our frappés in glasses that we will later deposit on the taverna's doorstep.

On our way back we are twice blessed — with the haphazard washing lines of octopus silhouettes and a Greek sunset.

Serves 4

1 WHOLE OCTOPUS
125 ml (½ cup) OLIVE OIL
3 TABLESPOONS RED WINE VINEGAR
1 TEASPOON DRIED OREGANO

GRILLED OCTOPUS WITH OREGANO

In Greece you will often see the whole octopus left hanging out in the sun to dry. Some cooks will also boil it for a bit before grilling on the barbecue, to ensure that it remains soft. So, if you can, hang your octopus out in the sun for a few hours beforehand, until the legs have dried and curled up a bit. I think this would go well with a fennel salad. And it is often served with a glass of ouzo on ice.

Heat the barbecue to hot. Cut the head off the octopus just below the eyes. Remove the beak by pushing it out through the centre of the tentacles. Cut the eyes from the head by slicing off a small round. Remove the intestines by pushing them out of the head. Rinse the octopus thoroughly.

Put the octopus on the barbecue and turn once there are a few charred bits (otherwise it will start to taste steamed). Remove to a serving platter and slice up into chunks.

Mix together the olive oil, vinegar and oregano and season with salt and pepper. Drizzle the dressing over the octopus and serve immediately.

Serves 4–6 as an antipasto or 3–4 as a light meal

1 kg (2 lb 4 oz) CALAMARI (preferably baby calamari)
100 g (3¹/₂ oz) BUTTER
JUICE OF 1¹/₂ LEMONS
3 GARLIC CLOVES, *finely chopped*
2 TABLESPOONS CHOPPED PARSLEY
LEMON WEDGES, *to serve*

CALAMARI
WITH BUTTER, LEMON
& GARLIC

This must be cooked in a really hot chargrill pan and then combined with the sauce to serve. You could also add a little chilli here if you like. Serve with white rice or pasta, or just bread to wipe up the buttery garlic.

To clean the calamari, pull the tentacles away from the body. Remove the transparent bone from inside the body and rinse the body well under cold running water. Holding the tentacles firmly with one hand, squeeze out the little beak and cut it away, leaving the tentacles whole. Rinse the tentacles. Cut the body into rings about 3 cm (about an inch) thick, leaving the tentacles whole (if they seem particularly large, cut them in half). Pat dry.

Heat the butter in a saucepan and, when it sizzles, add the lemon juice. Season with salt and pepper. Add the garlic and let it sizzle for a moment to flavour the butter but not burn. Stir in the parsley and remove from the heat.

Heat a ridged chargrill pan (griddle) to very hot (it should be just about smoking). Scatter with about half the calamari in a single layer (you will have to do it in two batches) and cook it over the highest possible heat. When you see that the calamari has darkened in parts on the underside, turn over with tongs and cook until the other side is darkened (take care that it doesn't burn though, or it will taste bitter). Move it around in the pan with a wooden spoon and let it cook for a couple of minutes more, then add it to the warm butter in the saucepan while you cook the next batch. Season to taste if necessary and serve hot, directly from the pan, with lemon wedges.

Serves 2–3

1 kg (2 lb 4 oz) SALT COD (BACCALA), *soaked in cold water
  for 2 days*
LIGHT OLIVE or CORN OIL, *for deep-frying*
90 g (3/4 cup) PLAIN (ALL-PURPOSE) FLOUR, *for dusting*
1/2 TEASPOON DRIED OREGANO
SKORDALIA (SEE OVER), *to serve*

DEEP-FRIED
SALT COD

If you can, soak the salt cod under a dripping tap so the water is constantly changing. If you can't manage that, soak it for two days, changing the water regularly. You can taste a small piece of the fish to see how salty it still is. Serve with skordalia. (I have also seen a dressing made with olive oil, lemon juice, oregano, salt and pepper poured over this fried fish.)

Dry the cod with kitchen paper and remove any bones. Cut into smaller portions (about 6 cm/2 1/2 inches). Half-fill a large saucepan or deep-fat fryer with oil and heat up for frying.

Dust the fish in the flour, shaking off any excess. Lower into the hot oil and deep-fry until crispy and golden. Take care as it becomes soft and can break. Lift out onto a plate lined with kitchen paper, patting on both sides to remove the excess oil. Transfer to a clean serving plate. Scatter with oregano, season with ground black pepper and serve with skordalia on the side.

Serves 10–12

1 LARGE CARROT, *cut in half*
1 SMALL CELERY STALK
A FEW PARSLEY STALKS
1 SMALL ONION
A FEW BLACK PEPPERCORNS
500 g (1 lb 2 oz) POTATOES, *peeled and cut into chunks*
5 GARLIC CLOVES
185 ml (3/4 cup) OLIVE OIL
JUICE OF 1 LEMON

SKORDALIA

When you are in the mood for garlic this is the thing. Some people make it with bread and vinegar instead of the potatoes and lemon. This is wonderful served with deep-fried salt cod.

Put the carrot, celery, parsley and onion in a fairly large saucepan of water, add some salt and a few peppercorns and bring to the boil. Boil for about 15 minutes before adding the potatoes and then boil for another 25 minutes or so, until the potatoes are very soft.

Meanwhile, crush the garlic completely with about 1 teaspoon of salt to make a purée. Put the garlic in a small bowl and add a couple of tablespoons of the olive oil.

Take out one third of the potatoes with a slotted spoon and mash in a large wide bowl with a potato masher or put through a food mill. Add the garlic, then mash another third of the potatoes with more of the olive oil and a little of the lemon juice. Carry on until you have used all the potatoes, lemon juice and olive oil and have a smooth purée. Taste for salt. The skordalia should have a fairly soft consistency and can be eaten with fried or grilled fish, meatballs or just on bread. Serve at room temperature.

Serves 6

1.5 kg (3 lb 5 oz) WHOLE OCTOPUS (*preferably
  with thick tentacles*)
140 ml (5 fl oz) OLIVE OIL
1 kg (2 lb 4 oz) SMALL STEWING ONIONS, *peeled and left whole*
1 TABLESPOON SUGAR
3 TABLESPOONS GOOD-QUALITY RED WINE VINEGAR
3 GARLIC CLOVES, *chopped*
450 g (1 lb) TIN PEELED TOMATOES, *roughly chopped*
375 ml (1¹/₂ cups) RED WINE
2 BAY LEAVES
1 SMALL DRIED RED CHILLI, *chopped*
A PINCH OF GRATED NUTMEG
1 CINNAMON STICK
A FEW ALLSPICE (PIMENTO) BERRIES

OCTOPUS STIFADO
(OCTOPUS WITH ONIONS & RED WINE)

This is a rich octopus and baby onion stew with red wine and spices. The same dish is also often made using rabbit or beef instead of the octopus (the cooking technique will vary slightly). It is important to let this dish sit for at least half an hour before serving as the onions will continue to cook in the hot casserole.

Cut the head off the octopus just below the eyes. Remove the beak by pushing it out through the centre of the tentacles. Cut the eyes from the head by slicing off a small round. Remove the intestines by pushing them out of the head. Rinse the head and tentacles thoroughly and cut up into chunks of about 3 cm (about an inch). Put the octopus pieces in a large pan, cover and cook over high heat for about 3 minutes. The octopus will create some liquid and brighten up a lot in colour. Stir now and then and cook, covered, for another 10 minutes until all the liquid has evaporated.

Meanwhile, heat 100 ml (3¹/₂ fl oz) of the olive oil in a large saucepan. Add the onions and sauté gently until softened, stirring now and then with a wooden spoon but taking care not to break them up. When they are lightly golden, add the sugar and vinegar and continue cooking until the sauce at the bottom of the pan thickens. The onions should be quite soft now.

Add the remaining olive oil and the garlic to the octopus and sauté for a few seconds more. Add the tomato and cook for 5 minutes. Add the wine, bay leaves, chilli, nutmeg, cinnamon and allspice. Season with salt and pepper. Add 750 ml (3 cups) water and bring to the boil. Lower the heat and simmer, uncovered, for about 30 minutes.

Add the onions, mix through gently, cover the pan and cook for another 30 minutes. Hold the pan and lid with a cloth in both hands and hula hoop the pan around occasionally so that it doesn't stick and the onions remain whole. The octopus and onions should be barely covered with a slightly thickened sauce, but add a little more hot water if it seems necessary. Remove from the heat, cover and leave to cool for about 30 minutes before serving. Serve warm, not piping hot, with your favourite bread and a salad.

Sisi's breakfasts

To this day I thank my mother for the unconventional breakfasts that she would serve as we grew up. In the mornings she would present us with leftover Greek lamb, prawns, stuffed vegetables... the recipes are all here in this book.

Serves 2–3

3–4 kg (about 6 1/2 lb) ROCK SALT
1 WHOLE FISH (about 1.2 kg/2 lb 11 oz) *gutted, scaled, rinsed*
    and dried with paper towels
2 LARGE HANDFULS FLAT-LEAF (ITALIAN) PARSLEY
    LEAVES, *rinsed and dried*
2 LEMONS
1/2 TEASPOON SWEET PAPRIKA
60 ml (1/4 cup) EXTRA VIRGIN OLIVE OIL

SALT-BAKED
FISH WITH LEMON &
PARSLEY SALAD

This just seems so healthy and can serve more or less, depending on the size of the fish. Use any fish you like, estimating that about 1 kg (2 lb 4 oz) of cleaned fish will be enough for two or three people. You might like to put a few sprigs of herbs or fennel leaves, a couple of bay leaves or lemon slices inside the cavity before cooking, although even with the fish completely plain this dish is really quite special.

Preheat your oven to 200°C (400°F/Gas 6). Put half of the salt in the bottom of an oven dish that is slightly larger than the fish but which still fits it quite snugly. Lay the fish on top, mounding the salt up a little over the sides of the fish. Cover the fish with the remaining salt, patting it firmly in place. Bake for about 35–40 minutes. To test if the fish is cooked, poke a skewer into the middle of it: the skewer should be hot when you pull it out. Transfer to a plate and crack open the salt crust. Fillet the fish into pieces that are as whole as you can manage.

While the fish is cooking, make the lemon and parsley salad. Put the whole parsley leaves in a bowl, making sure they don't have any tough stalks attached. To make lemon fillets, slice the tops and bottoms off the lemons. Sit the lemons on a board and, with a small sharp knife, cut downwards to remove the skin and pith. Holding the lemon over the bowl, remove the segments by slicing between the white pith. Remove any pips. Add the lemon fillets to the parsley and mix through the paprika and olive oil. Season with salt and pepper and squeeze out any juice from the lemon 'skeletons' over the salad.

Serve the fish with a small pile of salad on top and have an extra drizzle of olive oil handy in case anyone needs more.

Serves 6 or more

2 kg (4 lb 8 oz) LARGE RAW PRAWNS (SHRIMP), *unpeeled*
200 g (7 oz) BUTTER
10 GARLIC CLOVES, *finely chopped*
45 g (3/4 cup) CHOPPED PARSLEY
LESS THAN 1 TEASPOON PERI PERI SPICE *or* CHILLI
    POWDER
JUICE OF 4 LEMONS
400 g (14 oz) FETA CHEESE

PRAWNS WITH
LEMON, PERI PERI, GARLIC
& FETA

This is amazing. Everyone who has tasted this dish loves it and still now I use it for a special occasion dinner — it seems very 'celebration'. My mother still salts every single prawn individually; once she has slit and removed the dark line of the prawn she sprinkles salt along this. You can just scatter salt over each layer in the saucepan. My mother always uses peri peri, which is a wonderfully flavoured full-potency chilli that we get in South Africa. Substitute your favourite chilli powder or cayenne pepper, using as much as you like. I like a good balance of strong flavours but the chilli should not be too overpowering. You can clean the prawns beforehand and keep them covered in a colander in the fridge, then you'll only need about 20 minutes before serving. This dish needs very little else — bread, some white rice or couscous and a large green salad.

Clean the prawns and cut a slit through the shell down the back from the bottom of the head to the beginning of the tail. Remove the dark vein with the point of a sharp knife. Rinse the prawns under running water and drain well.

Dot about 80 g (2³/4 oz) of the butter over the base of a large cast-iron casserole dish. Arrange a single layer of prawns in the dish and season with salt. Scatter about a third of the garlic and parsley over the top. Sprinkle with a little of the peri peri.

Dot about half of the remaining butter over the top and arrange another layer of prawns, scattered with garlic, parsley and peri peri. Repeat the layer, finishing up the ingredients. Put the lid on, turn the heat to medium-high and cook for about 10 minutes, until the prawns have brightened up a lot and their flesh is white. Add the lemon juice, crumble the feta over the top and rock the dish from side to side to move the sauce about. Spoon some sauce over the prawns. Cover the casserole, lower the heat and cook for another 10 minutes or until the feta has just melted, shaking the pan again. Take the dish straight to the table and give everyone a hot finger bowl with lemon juice to clean their hands afterwards.

Serves 4–6

1 kg (2 lb 4 oz) FIRM WHITE FISH FILLETS,
  cut into 6 cm (2¹/2 inch) pieces
400 g (14 oz) TIN TOMATOES WITH JUICE,
  chopped (or VERY RIPE TOMATOES, *peeled and chopped*)
15 g (¹/4 cup) CHOPPED PARSLEY
4 LARGE GARLIC CLOVES, *finely chopped*
JUICE OF 2 LEMONS
2 CELERY STALKS, *chopped, with some leaves*
1 TEASPOON SUGAR
3 TABLESPOONS OLIVE OIL
CRUSTY BREAD, *to serve*

OVEN-BAKED
FISH WITH TOMATO
& PARSLEY

This is great served either hot or cold, even straight from the fridge. It is wonderful with boiled potatoes that you have sprinkled with parsley and drizzled with a little olive oil. Actually, you could just put some boiled potatoes around the fish in the juice once you have removed the foil. Use any type of fresh fish fillets you like.

Preheat the oven to 180°C (350°F/Gas 4). Put the fish in an oven dish where they will fit in a single layer. Mix together the tomatoes, parsley, garlic, lemon juice, celery, sugar and olive oil and taste for seasoning. Pour over the fish to cover all the pieces, shaking the dish from side to side. Cover with foil and bake for about 30 minutes.

Remove the aluminium foil, increase the heat to 200°C (400°F/Gas 6) and bake for another 40–50 minutes, or until the liquid has thickened and the top of the fish is golden in a couple of places. Serve with crusty bread to mop up the juices.

Serves 2–3

1 SMALL CHICKEN
2 TABLESPOONS OLIVE OIL
50 g (1³/4 oz) BUTTER
JUICE OF 2 LEMONS
1 TABLESPOON DRIED OREGANO

LEMON & OREGANO CHICKEN

These are very familiar flavours to me and I don't ever tire of them. I love the simplicity of something that you can throw under the grill while you put together a salad and set the table. You could cook this on a barbecue, varying the herbs, or you could cook it from start to finish under the grill, leaving out the frying. But this is how my friends Corinne and Liz cook their chicken, and I think it gives it extra crispiness and flavour.

Preheat the grill (broiler) to high. Put the chicken breast-side down and cut along the backbone. Turn the chicken over and push down firmly to butterfly and flatten it.

Heat the olive oil and 30 g (1 oz) of the butter in a large frying pan. Add the chicken and half the lemon juice, season with salt and cook until both sides are crispy and the chicken is just cooked through. Put the chicken on a baking tray. Pour over the remaining lemon juice, dot with the remaining butter and sprinkle with the oregano, crushing it between your fingers.

Pour 125 ml (¹/2 cup) of water around the chicken and grill (broil) it on both sides until the top is crispy and deep golden. Pour a little more water around the chicken and grill for a bit longer so that you have some sauce.

Cut the chicken into pieces to serve, seasoning with a little more salt if necessary. Serve hot or at room temperature, with the sauce, bread and a green salad.

Serves 4–6

3 TABLESPOONS OLIVE OIL
800 g (1 lb 12 oz) LAMB MEAT (from shoulder or leg),
  trimmed and cut into 3 cm (1¼ inch) pieces
2 RED ONIONS, *finely chopped*
2 GARLIC CLOVES, *chopped*
600 g (1 lb 5 oz) TINNED TOMATOES *with juice, chopped*
1 PIECE OF CASSIA BARK *or* CINNAMON
30 g (1 oz) BUTTER
400 g (14 oz) RISONI *or* ORZO
GRATED PARMESAN, PECORINO *or* KEFALOTIRI
  CHEESE, *to serve*

YOUVETSI
(LAMB & TOMATO
WITH RICE-SHAPED NOODLES)

Some people like to serve this with cubes of feta or haloumi stirred in at the end so that they melt a bit. Risoni or orzo pasta is like a large grain of rice and you can use any small noodle instead, although the cooking time will probably vary. If you prefer, use one big piece of meat on the bone instead of cubes, and just break it up into portions for serving. The meat must be very soft, so cook it as long as it needs before adding the pasta to the casserole for the last 15 minutes.

Preheat the oven to 180°C (350°F/Gas 4). Heat the olive oil in a heavy casserole and fry the lamb in batches until golden on all sides. Transfer the meat to a plate and add the onions to the casserole. Sauté the onions until golden and softened, stirring all the time so they don't stick (you can add another drop of oil). Add the garlic and cook for another half a minute or so before returning the meat to the pan. Add the tomatoes, crushing them with a wooden spoon, season with salt and pepper and add the cassia or cinnamon and the butter. Let it all bubble up for 5 minutes or so and then add 1 litre (4 cups) hot water. Cover and bake for 1 hour or until the lamb is tender.

Rinse the pasta in a fine sieve or colander, drain and add to the casserole. Mix through, cover and return it to the oven for another 15 minutes, or until the pasta is cooked and has absorbed most of the sauce. The cooking time will depend on the pasta — it takes longer to cook in the oven, so pasta that needs 7 minutes on the stovetop will take 15 minutes in the oven. You may need to add a little more hot water if it seems too dry. Serve hot, sprinkled with the grated cheese.

If you are not serving this immediately, remove the casserole from the oven before the pasta is completely cooked — the residual heat in the casserole dish will finish off the cooking.

Serves 6

1.5 kg (3 lb 5 oz) LEG OF LAMB (on the bone)
JUICE OF 2 LEMONS
1 TABLESPOON DRIED OREGANO
50 g (13/4 oz) BUTTER
3 TABLESPOONS OLIVE OIL
4 LARGE POTATOES

LEG OF LAMB WITH OREGANO & LEMON

This is possibly one of my favourite meals. It is soft, wonderful and meltingly lemony and we would sometimes eat the leftovers for breakfast before school. I'm not sure if this is totally the Greek way of making it — maybe the butter and cooking time are my mother's addition — but this is how it is. My mother says you could cook it overnight: I never have, but I believe her.

Preheat the oven to 220°C (425°F/Gas 7). Rinse and trim the lamb of excess fat and put it in a large baking dish. Rub the lamb all over with the lemon juice, season well with salt and pepper and sprinkle with the oregano, crushing it between your fingers to cover the meat. Dot the butter over the top. Pour 250 ml (1 cup) water around the lamb and drizzle the olive oil around it as well. Bake for about 15–30 minutes on each side, until it is browned all over.

Meanwhile, peel the potatoes and cut them into bite-sized pieces. Scatter them in the baking dish around the browned lamb, add some salt and turn them over with a wooden spoon to coat them in the juice. Add a little more water if it has evaporated. Cover the baking tray with foil, lower the heat to 180°C (350°F/Gas 4) and bake for 2½ hours or so, turning the lamb over at least once during this time and shuffling the potatoes. If the lamb isn't browned enough, remove the foil for the final 30 minutes of cooking. Serve warm on a huge platter with a salad or some simply cooked greens. This is also nice with some tzatziki on the side.

Serves 6

4–5 TABLESPOONS OLIVE OIL
2 ONIONS, *chopped*
1.25 kg (2 lb 12 oz) BONELESS LEG OF PORK,
 cut into 5 cm (2 inch) *chunks*
2 GARLIC CLOVES, *lightly crushed*
250 ml (1 cup) WHITE WINE
1 LARGE HEAD OF CELERY
1 TEASPOON DRIED WILD FENNEL FLOWERS
3 EGGS
JUICE OF 2 LEMONS

PORK
WITH CELERY IN EGG &
LEMON SAUCE

This is a dish that's good served on its own with some bread. If you don't have dried fennel flowers, add a couple of soft branches of wild fennel or dill.

Heat 3 tablespoons of the olive oil in a large heavy-based saucepan over medium heat. Add the onions and sauté until softened. Add a little extra oil, then add the pork pieces to the pan and continue cooking until the meat browns a bit. Add the garlic and cook for another minute. Add the wine and leave to reduce a bit. Season with salt and pepper, add 750 ml (3 cups) of water and bring to the boil. Lower the heat and simmer for 1 hour. Check the water level of the meat occasionally — it should be simmering in some liquid, so add more if necessary.

Trim the celery and separate all the stalks. Chop off the top leafy parts (you won't need them here). Strip away the stringy bits with a knife, starting at the bottom and pulling all the way to the top so that the strings come away. Cut the stalks into lengths of about 5 cm (2 inches).

Add the celery and dried fennel to the pan with another 750 ml (3 cups) of hot water. Cover and simmer for another 45 minutes or so, again checking the water level and adding a bit more if necessary. Remove the pan from the heat and leave for 5 minutes.

Whisk the eggs in a bowl with some salt and pepper. Whisk a ladleful of the meat juices into the eggs, whisking continuously to make sure they don't scramble. Add another ladleful of juice and then pour the eggs into the saucepan, mixing with a wooden spoon. Add the lemon juice and mix through. Put the pan back onto the lowest heat possible and cook for another minute or so, stirring continuously to just cook and thicken the eggs. Remove from the heat, taste for seasoning and serve immediately.

Serves 6–8

900 g (2 lb) MINCED (GROUND) BEEF AND PORK
2 LARGE RED ONIONS, *finely grated*
15 g (1/2 cup) CHOPPED PARSLEY
250 g (11/3 cups) UNCOOKED SHORT-GRAIN RICE
4 TABLESPOONS OLIVE OIL, PLUS 125 ml (1/2 cup) EXTRA
1 HEAPED TEASPOON SWEET PAPRIKA
1 TEASPOON DRIED MINT, *crumbled*
1 TEASPOON GROUND PEPPER
2 TEASPOONS SALT
6–8 RIPE TOMATOES
4 PEPPERS (CAPSICUMS)
4 ZUCCHINI (COURGETTES)
4 POTATOES, *cut in half lengthways and then into halves or thirds*
3 TABLESPOONS BUTTER, *melted*
JUICE OF HALF A LEMON

STUFFED VEGETABLES

This is a wonderful colourful tray of mixed vegetables, which you can vary according to what's easily available and in season (you could use only tomatoes or try mixed colours of peppers). These can be made in advance and served at room temperature or warmed up before serving if you prefer. I've used a combination of tomatoes, peppers and zucchini, which can be halved or divided, so that everyone gets a taste of each.

Preheat the oven to 200°C (400°F/Gas 6). Put the meat in a large bowl with the onions, parsley, rice, 4 tablespoons of oil, paprika, mint, pepper and salt.

Slice the tops off the tomatoes and keep them on one side. Hollow out the insides of the tomatoes with a teaspoon (a pointed one is easiest), holding them over a bowl to catch the juice. Chop up the pulp and add to the meat with half of the juice from the tomatoes. Keep the rest of the juice. Sit the tomatoes on a large oven tray.

Cut away a top hat from each pepper, leaving a hinge of a couple of centimetres (3/4 inch) on one side. Scoop out the seeds and throw them away, but save any of the fleshy pepper bits that you can. Chop up this flesh and add it to the meat. Put the peppers on the tray — it doesn't matter if they don't sit flat, they can lie down.

Meanwhile, heat the remaining oil and garlic in a large non-stick saucepan. Add the eggplant flesh, celery and paprika and sauté over medium heat until it is softened and very lightly golden. Add the minced meat and continue cooking for 10–15 minutes, until the meat is lightly golden, seasoning lightly with salt. Break up any clusters of meat with a wooden spoon. Mix in 250 ml (1 cup) of the cooked tomato sauce, cook for 2–3 minutes more and then remove from the heat to cool slightly. If your pan is big enough, mix in the parmesan, feta, and parsley — if not, mix it all together in a larger bowl. Check the seasoning. Remove the garlic clove from the tomato sauce.

Ladle tomato sauce onto the bottom of a baking dish to a depth of 2 cm (3/4 inch). Use a dish that is large enough to fit all the eggplants fairly compactly in a single layer. Fill the eggplant boats with meat filling, patting it in well with your hands, but don't make it too compact. Arrange the eggplants on top of the tomato sauce and splash the tops with the rest of the tomato sauce, but don't drown them.

Bake for 30–45 minutes (or longer if necessary) until the sauce is bubbling up and a little bit of a golden crust has formed on the top in places. Remove from the oven and cool slightly before serving. These are also good served at room temperature.

Serves 8 as a side dish

500 g (1 lb 2 oz) DRIED BUTTER BEANS (LIMA BEANS),
  soaked overnight
1 BAY LEAF
125 ml (1/2 cup) OLIVE OIL
2 SMALL RED ONIONS, *finely chopped*
2 CELERY STALKS WITH LEAVES, *chopped*
3 GARLIC CLOVES, *finely chopped*
650 g (1 lb 7 oz) RIPE TOMATOES, *peeled and coarsely grated*
  (or use tinned)
4 TABLESPOONS CHOPPED PARSLEY
3 TABLESPOONS BREADCRUMBS

BAKED BUTTER BEANS
WITH ONIONS, TOMATOES
& PARSLEY

This is a good companion for any roast or grilled meat dish and it can also stand alone as a vegetarian option, served with some sautéed greens and a small dish of feta. You could even stir through some freshly chopped dill before baking.

Drain the beans, put them in a saucepan with the bay leaf, cover generously with cold water and bring to the boil. Skim off any scum that rises, lower the heat slightly and cook for about 1 1/2 hours or until they are very tender. Add salt towards the end of the cooking time.

Preheat the oven to 180°C (350°F/Gas 4). Drain the beans, keeping about 375 ml (1 1/2 cups) of the cooking water, and put them in a large baking dish.

Heat about 2 tablespoons of the olive oil in a non-stick frying pan. Gently sauté the onions until they are lightly golden and softened, stirring so that they don't stick. Remove from the heat and mix in a bowl with the celery, garlic, tomatoes, parsley and remaining olive oil. Season with pepper and a little salt. Add the reserved bean water, pour all this into the beans and mix through well. Cover with foil and bake for about 45 minutes, then remove the foil and stir the beans, adding a little extra water if they seem to be drying out. Sprinkle with breadcrumbs and return to the oven, uncovered, for another 30 minutes.

The beans should be tender, golden on the top and still with a little sauce. Serve warm, with an extra drizzling of olive oil if you like.

Serves 8 as a side dish

1 RED ONION, *very thinly sliced*
1 TEASPOON SALT
1.5 kg (3 lb 5 oz) WAXY POTATOES
3 TABLESPOONS DRAINED BABY CAPERS
30 g (1/2 cup) CHOPPED PARSLEY
JUICE OF 1 1/2 LEMONS
100 g (about 1/2 cup) GOOD-QUALITY BLACK OLIVES
125 ml (1/2 cup) EXTRA VIRGIN OLIVE OIL

BOILED
POTATO SALAD

This is great for an outdoor lunch that you can just do ahead and take with you wherever you are going. Use waxy potatoes if possible. You could add some mashed up hard-boiled eggs and anchovies here too, or any other ingredients you think would go nicely.

Put the onion in a small bowl and cover with cold water and the salt. Leave for 30 minutes or so (while you prepare the potatoes). The soaking is important and will give your onions a softer taste in the finished dish and make them more digestible.

Scrub the potatoes and boil in salted water for about 20–25 minutes until they are cooked but not falling apart. Drain well, then peel them when they have cooled a little — it is easier to do this if they are still warm. Cut them into chunks the size that you would like to see in your salad bowl.

Rinse the onion and drain well, patting it dry with kitchen paper if necessary. Add to the potato with the remaining ingredients, seasoning with pepper and probably a little extra salt. Mix through gently and serve warm or at room temperature. If you make this in advance, the potatoes will soak up some of the oil as they cool, so you will have less dressing. You could save a little of the oil and add it closer to the serving time, if more is needed.

Remove the vanilla bean from the semolina mixture, scraping out all the seeds into the pan with a knife. Take 2 tablespoons of the melted butter and stir it into the semolina with the beaten eggs. Pour this over the filo layers in your ovenproof dish and cover with seven more layers of pastry (14 sheets), brushing each sheet with the melted butter as before.

Trim all the edges of the pastry, leaving a small overhang on all sides. Fold all the edges neatly onto the custard. Cut one more sheet of filo to exactly fit the top of the dish and hide the tucked-in edges. Brush this with melted butter.

This bit is tricky. Using a very sharp knife, score serving portions like a grid on the surface of the pastry, cutting through a couple of layers of the filo (it will be almost impossible to do this neatly after it is cooked). To prevent the pastry moving about too much and the custard leaking out, support it with your free hand as you cut. You should get about 20 small servings.

Bake in the middle of the oven for 15 minutes. Reduce the temperature to 150°C (300°F/Gas 2) and bake for another 45 minutes. Remove from the oven, dust the surface with icing sugar and then cinnamon and then return to the oven for 10 minutes. Leave to cool slightly before cutting into the serving portions.

Serves 8

syrup
80 g (2³/4 oz) CASTER (SUPERFINE) SUGAR
2 TABLESPOONS RUNNY HONEY
¹/2 TEASPOON GROUND CINNAMON
3 CLOVES
JUICE OF HALF A SMALL LEMON

6 SHEETS FILO PASTRY
150 g (5¹/2 oz) BUTTER, *melted*
125 g (4¹/2 oz) GOOD-QUALITY, SOFT DRIED APRICOTS
40 g (¹/4 cup) WHOLE ALMONDS, *roughly chopped*
40 g (1 ¹/2 oz) SKINNED, UNSALTED PISTACHIO NUTS,
    roughly chopped
1 EGG WHITE
30 g (1 oz) CASTER (SUPERFINE) SUGAR
A FEW DROPS OF VANILLA EXTRACT

BAKLAVA WITH NUTS &
DRIED APRICOTS

This is how Corinne and Lizzie made their baklava. I learnt a lot of their recipes as one night, when their restaurant was very full, they pulled me out of my chair and put me to work. I stayed quite a while. The quantities given here are very simple to double or adjust. Serve this warm with cinnamon or vanilla ice cream.

To make the syrup, put all the ingredients in a saucepan with 185 ml (³/4 cup) water, bring to the boil and boil for 5 minutes or so, until it is clear and slightly thickened. Remove from the heat and leave to cool completely.

Preheat the oven to 180°C (350°F/Gas 4). Lay a sheet of filo on the work surface and brush generously with melted butter. Top with a second sheet of filo and brush with butter. Repeat with a third sheet of filo, brushing the top with butter. Cut the filo into four equal strips along its length. Do the same with the remaining sheets of filo, so you have eight strips in total.

Finely chop the apricots in a food processor. Mix the apricots and nuts in a bowl and taste to see if it is sweet enough — mix some sugar through if the apricots taste a bit sour. You should have a moist rough paste.

Whip the egg white in a bowl until soft peaks form and then whisk in the sugar and vanilla. Continue whisking until stiff and creamy.

Take a heaped tablespoon of the apricot mixture and press onto one strip of the filo about 7 cm (3 inches) up from the bottom edge. Put a heaped teaspoon of the egg white over the apricot mix, and then fold the bottom of the pastry up over the filling. Turn in both the sides, pressing these down all the way up the length. Then roll up to make a neat package and seal the filling in. Brush with melted butter and put on a tray lined with baking paper. Repeat with the rest of the pastry and filling. Bake for 15–20 minutes until the pastry is crisp and golden.

Arrange the baklava on a serving plate. Pour the cool syrup over the hot baklava and serve warm with a scoop of not-too-sweet vanilla ice cream, spooning any extra syrup over the baklava. These can also be eaten cold.

The villages of Greece and the islands are so beautiful around Easter, with everyone holding onto their candles in church at midnight. On the Sunday just about every soul around eats lamb, either turned on the spit or oven-roasted.

We loved the part when we would crack our red-dyed, hard-boiled eggs against each other to find out which was the strongest.

Serves 8

5 ORANGES
3 SHEETS FILO PASTRY
60 g (2¹/4 oz) BUTTER, *melted*
30 g (1 oz) SUGAR
3 TABLESPOONS RUNNY HONEY

orange confit
GRATED RIND AND JUICE OF 1 ORANGE
30 g (1 oz) SUGAR

orange sauce
JUICE OF 3 ORANGES
15 g (¹/2 oz) BUTTER
30 g (1 oz) SUGAR
1 TABLESPOON GRAND MARNIER, PORT
  or VIN SANTO

sabayon cream
1 x 2 g GELATINE LEAF
1 EGG, PLUS 2 EGG YOLKS
50 g (1³/4 oz) SUGAR
1 TEASPOON ORANGE BLOSSOM WATER
300 ml (10¹/2 fl oz) WHIPPING CREAM

ICING (CONFECTIONERS') SUGAR, *to serve*

FILO
MILLEFEUILLE
WITH ORANGES

This always reminds me of Athens and the avenues lined with orange trees. I have also made this with pomegranates, juicing one or two and following the same method for the orange sauce here. Or use both and scatter pomegranate seeds and orange slices around the plate: the colours look beautiful together.

Slice the tops and bottoms off the oranges. To fillet the oranges, sit them on a board. With a small sharp knife, cut downwards to remove the skin and pith. Hold the orange over a bowl and remove the fillets by slicing in between the white pith. Remove the pips. You should be left with an orange 'skeleton'. Put the fillets in the bowl and squeeze out the remaining juice from the skeletons, then discard the skeletons.

To make the orange confit, put the ingredients in a small saucepan and simmer for 7–8 minutes, until a jam forms.

To make the sauce, put all the ingredients in a saucepan and pour in the juice from the orange fillets as well. Boil until thickened and reduced.

To make the sabayon cream, put the gelatine in a small bowl (you can snap the leaf if necessary), cover with cold water and leave it to soften completely. Put the whole egg, egg yolks and sugar in a heatproof bowl over a saucepan of simmering water, making sure the bottom of the bowl isn't touching the water. Whisk constantly for about 12–15 minutes or until the mixture is thick and fluffy.

Whisk in 2 teaspoons of the confit and the orange blossom water and take the bowl off the saucepan. (If there's any confit left you can add it to the cream or oranges at the last minute, or serve it over ice cream.)

Squeeze out all the water from the gelatine with your hands and whisk the gelatine into the sabayon cream, making sure it is well incorporated. Now whip the cream to soft peaks and fold this into the sabayon. Leave in a cool place, even in the fridge, until you are ready to use it.

Preheat the oven to 180°C (350°F/Gas 4). Place a sheet of filo pastry on a work surface, brush with melted butter and sprinkle the surface evenly with half the sugar. Place another sheet of filo on the first, brush with butter and sprinkle with the remaining sugar. Add the last sheet of filo, brushing with butter. Cut the filo in half horizontally and then cut each half into 12 strips, giving you a total of 24 rectangles. Put them on a baking tray lined with baking paper, drizzle the honey in long thin lines all over the filo and bake for 10 minutes, or until crisp and golden brown. Set aside to cool on a clean sheet of baking paper so that they don't stick.

To serve, place a filo rectangle on each plate. Add a good dollop of sabayon cream, a few orange slices, another layer of filo, more sabayon and orange segments and a final layer of filo. Scatter a few orange segments around the plate, drizzle with sauce, dust the top with icing sugar and serve.

Makes 45

250 g (9 oz) BUTTER
2 TABLESPOONS ICING (CONFECTIONERS') SUGAR,
   PLUS ABOUT 300 g (10^1/2 oz), *for dusting*
1 EGG YOLK
1 TEASPOON VANILLA EXTRACT
1 TABLESPOON BRANDY
300 g (10^1/2 oz) CAKE FLOUR *or* PLAIN (ALL-PURPOSE)
   FLOUR, *sifted*
1 TEASPOON BAKING POWDER

KOURAPIEDES

These really do melt in your mouth. You can serve them on their own with tea, coffee, a liqueur or just a glass of iced water. Sometimes I like to make up a dessert plate: a small pile of these, little baklava and a tiny glass of preserved fruits in sugar syrup. You will find you really have to eat these over a plate or pop a whole one in your mouth at once so that the icing sugar doesn't fly everywhere. You will use a lot of icing sugar for dusting: you can always recycle some from the bottom, or sieve the leftover sugar of crumbs and put it back in your tin.

Preheat the oven to 180°C (350°F/Gas 4) and line a baking tray with a sheet of baking paper.

Using electric beaters, beat the butter for 8–10 minutes until it is very pale and thick. Add the 2 tablespoons of icing sugar, beating it in well. Add the egg yolk and vanilla and whisk until well incorporated, then mix in the brandy. Sift in the flour and baking powder, mixing until you have a thick dough that becomes difficult to mix with the electric mixer. Scoop up softly in your hands, cover in plastic wrap and refrigerate for about 30 minutes.

Form the dough into small balls about the size of cherry tomatoes (these are often made into crescent shapes too) and put them on the tray, leaving a little space between them.

Bake for about 20 minutes or until they are lightly golden. Remove from the oven and leave to cool for 10–15 minutes. Meanwhile, line another tray with baking paper and sprinkle with half of the icing sugar. Take the slightly cooled biscuits and place them in one layer on top of the icing sugar. Sprinkle the rest of the icing sugar over the top (the biscuits should be almost buried in the sugar). Keep these in an airtight container.

Serves 4

230 g (1 cup) CASTER (SUPERFINE)
  SUGAR
1 LONG STRIP LEMON RIND
JUICE OF HALF A LEMON
4 QUINCES

POACHED QUINCES

I like these with pistachio ice cream. I love the colour of the quinces after they have been gently stewing in their syrup for a couple of hours. You could add other flavourings with the fruit, such as half a vanilla bean, a piece of cinnamon stick, or perhaps some cloves.

Put the sugar, lemon rind, juice and about 1 litre (4 cups) of water in a saucepan and bring to the boil.

Meanwhile, cut the quinces into quarters from the top down. Core and peel them (take care with the knife that it doesn't slip on the hard quince). Halve the quince pieces now into slices of about 2 cm (3/4 inch) each and put them in the boiling syrup. Lower the heat to the lowest simmer possible, cover and simmer for about 2 hours. Add another 250 ml (1 cup) of water after about 45 minutes and another towards the end or if the syrup looks too scant. Try not to move the quinces about at all so that they don't break up. If you do need to move them, slide a wooden spoon under to shift them. When they are a beautiful colour, remove from the heat and leave them to cool in their syrup.

Serve the quinces with a little syrup drizzled over and a scoop of vanilla or pistachio ice cream (page 140).

Serves 8

3 TABLESPOONS RAISINS
4 TABLESPOONS GOOD BRANDY
4 QUINCES
3 TABLESPOONS SHELLED WALNUTS, *chopped*
1 TEASPOON GROUND CINNAMON
100 g (3¹/₂ oz) BROWN SUGAR
40 g (1¹/₂ oz) BUTTER, *diced*

BAKED QUINCES WITH BROWN SUGAR, CINNAMON & WALNUTS

This is more or less the way Ketty makes her quinces. She is a special cook and has a wonderful restaurant in Plaka, Athens, called Café Avissinia. You could serve these with pistachio or vanilla ice cream or a dollop of thick cream or crème fraiche.

Preheat the oven to 180°C (350°F/Gas 4). Put the raisins in a small bowl with the brandy and leave to soak for a bit.

Cut the quinces in half, leaving their skins on, and core them, making a nice nest where the core was. Put them in an ovenproof dish where they will fit compactly in a single layer. Spoon the raisins evenly into the nests and then drizzle the brandy over the top. Spoon the walnuts, cinnamon, brown sugar and butter into the nests. Pour 250 ml (1 cup) water into the dish and then cover with aluminium foil. Bake for about 2 hours, adding another 250 ml (1 cup) of hot water halfway through the cooking time and scraping up any bits of sugar or nuts that may be stuck to the edge of the dish. If it appears to need more water, add a little.

After about 2 hours the quinces should be really soft, but not collapsing, and beautifully golden with some thickened sauce. Serve warm, drizzled with some sauce.

Makes 750 ml (3 cups)

100 g (²/₃ cup) SHELLED UNSALTED
  PISTACHIO NUTS (200 g/7 oz unshelled)
250 ml (1 cup) MILK
400 ml (14 fl oz) POURING (single) CREAM
1 TABLESPOON GOOD BRANDY
4 EGG YOLKS
120 g (4 oz) CASTER (superfine) SUGAR

PISTACHIO ICE CREAM

You could serve this with a shard or crumblings of pistachio praline scattered on top or a nice chunk of dark chocolate. I like it with beautiful red quinces, either baked or poached in syrup. Make sure your pistachios are a lovely bright green to start with. You won't need the egg whites here, so save them in your freezer for another time.

Peel the reddish-brown skins from the pistachios to reveal the bright green nuts. (If the skins won't come away easily, drop the nuts into boiling water for a minute or so and then drain and peel them.) Put the nuts in a blender and pulse into coarse bits. Transfer them to a saucepan with the milk, cream and brandy and bring just to a rolling boil. Remove from the heat and, with a hand-held mixer, purée until fairly smooth. (It won't get completely smooth, and this will give your ice cream some texture.)

Whisk the egg yolks and sugar together for about 5 minutes until pale and creamy. Stir in a ladleful of the hot pistachio cream to acclimatise the eggs and then gradually add the rest. Return the mixture to the saucepan over very low heat and stir constantly for 4–5 minutes until it thickens. (Do not have the heat too high or the eggs will scramble.)

Remove the custard from the heat and leave it to cool completely, whisking every now and then to prevent the eggs from scrambling. Transfer to a bowl, cover and put in the freezer.

After an hour, remove the bowl from the freezer, give an energetic whisk with a hand whisk or electric mixer and return the bowl to the freezer. Whisk again after another couple of hours. When it is nearly firm, give one last whisk, transfer to a suitable freezing container with a lid and let it set in the freezer until it is firm.

Alternatively, pour the mixture into your ice-cream machine and freeze, following the manufacturer's instructions.

Serves 8–12

400 g (14 oz) SUGAR
1 HEAPED TEASPOON GROUND CINNAMON
ABOUT 4 CLOVES
JUICE OF HALF A LEMON
250 g (9 oz) BUTTER
350 g (12 oz) FINE SEMOLINA
115 g (1 cup) COARSELY GROUND WALNUTS

HALVA

There are three types of halva that I know of: one is a solid marble-looking block that is sold by the slice; the next is a semolina-type cake with nuts that is baked and then has a syrup poured over; this third kind is also with semolina, but cooked completely on the stovetop and then poured into a cake tin or ring. When cool it is cut into slices and has a very familiar taste and texture to me. You may find it unusual — to me its taste holds such history. It is a standard dish that any Greek lady would have a recipe for.

Lightly butter a bundt pan or 11 x 18 x 7 cm (5 x 7 x 3 inch) cake tin. To make the syrup, put the sugar, cinnamon, cloves, lemon juice and 1 litre (4 cups) of water in a saucepan and bring slowly to the boil to dissolve the sugar. Simmer for 10 minutes, or until syrupy. Remove from the heat.

Melt the butter in a large wide saucepan over medium heat and then cook for 3–4 minutes until it starts to turn golden and smells beautifully buttery (this is important for the final taste of the halva). Add the semolina and mix in well with a wooden spoon. Continue cooking for about 10 minutes, stirring and turning the semolina almost continuously so that it turns golden brown and doesn't burn. Add the nuts and cook for about 5 minutes, until they seem to have taken on a colour and the mixture smells nutty and buttery. Remove from the heat.

Return the syrup to the stove for a minute to heat through. Scoop out and discard the cloves. Carefully pour the hot syrup into the semolina (standing back a bit as it will splash up). The mixture will thicken in the pan, so stir vigorously with a wooden spoon until it comes away from the side of the pan. As it starts to look like a smooth thick porridge, pour it into the cake tin. Leave to cool completely, before turning out onto a plate. Serve in slices, sprinkled with a little extra cinnamon if you like.

CINNAMON + ROSES

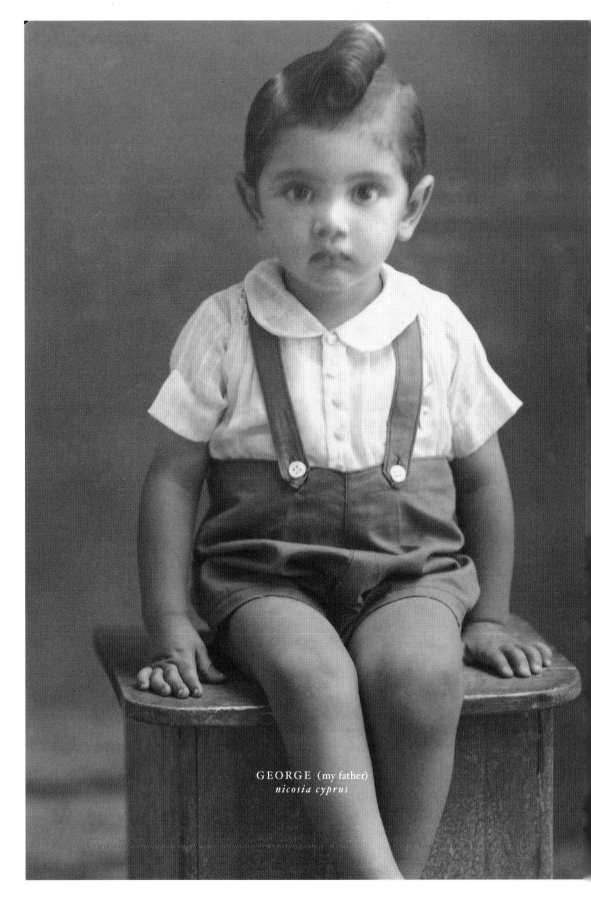

GEORGE (my father)
nicosia cyprus

Cyprus

CINNAMON + ROSES

Pappou, my special grandfather, was an ironmonger by trade and definitely a cook at heart. He was responsible for certain dishes in the household, which nobody interfered with. These were the souvlakia, souvla and all barbecues, when he would sit outside for ages turning the meat around and around. The salad, too, was his section, and so were those beautiful chips that had a method to their seeming madness. Pappou gave me his recipes, with measurements such as 'one flat woodenspoonful of sugar', as he stirred.

My grandfather would water his roses at any odd hour of night and had the same enthusiasm for every single thing he did, whether it was bashing his chips or driving my cousins to their music lesson in his beautiful old mini. I loved the smell and the sound of that long straw broom that he used to sweep the courtyard. That strong swish-swoshing sound of straw sweeping on cement and the smell of water that lullabied me to sleep some afternoons under the shade of the vines.

Serves 1

185 g (3/4 cup) NOT-TOO-THICK PLAIN
   YOGHURT
125 ml (^{1}/2 cup) ICE-COLD WATER
1 TEASPOON DRIED MINT
ABOUT ^{1}/2 TEASPOON SALT
CRUSHED ICE

AIRANI

In the summer, street vendors sell glasses of this in the old centre of Cyprus and I am not sure that there is anything else quite so refreshing. The salt really brings out the flavours. It may be an acquired taste, but I love it every now and then on a really hot day. You could also serve something like this as a cold summer soup, perhaps adding some diced cucumber.

Mix together the yoghurt, water and mint and season with the salt, checking for flavour and adjusting the salt to your taste. Scatter the crushed ice over the top and serve.

jasmine

The smell that hit you upon arrival in Nicosia was those jasmine bushes flanking the front door. Their syrupy delicate fragrance waltzed smoothly with the summer night heat. We would lie on the marble floors, soothing our bodies, hoping that some cooler air would arrive from somewhere. Still now, when I smell jasmine at night, I feel I could embrace the moon.

Serves 1

20 g (3/4 oz) BUTTER
1/2 TABLESPOON OLIVE OIL
1 SLICE HALOUMI CHEESE, *about* 2.5 cm (1 inch) *thick*
A LITTLE PLAIN (ALL-PURPOSE) FLOUR, *for dusting*
2 TABLESPOONS OUZO
HALF A LEMON

FRIED HALOUMI CHEESE

You can try this with any type of firm cheese. The nice thing about haloumi is that it holds its shape while just softening beautifully, instead of melting away. Make the slices as thick as you want. This can be cooked without the ouzo as part of a mixed meze, but on its own it stands beautifully with the flavour of the ouzo. Serve it simply in the pan you have cooked it in (if you have a small one), perhaps with a glass of ouzo on ice. I think it goes nicely with tzatziki too. To serve more people, just multiply the amounts.

Heat the butter and oil in a small frying pan over medium heat. Dust the haloumi with flour on both sides, shaking off the excess. Add to the hot pan and fry until golden on both sides, taking care that the butter doesn't burn. Then add the ouzo and carefully set it alight, standing back. Serve immediately with a squeeze of lemon.

Makes about 60 small meatballs

2 SLICES OF BREAD
125 ml (¹/₂ cup) MILK
700 g (1 lb 9 oz) MINCED (GROUND) PORK AND BEEF
¹/₂ TEASPOON DRIED MINT
2 TABLESPOONS CHOPPED FLAT-LEAF (ITALIAN)
  PARSLEY
2 EGGS
1 SWEET APPLE, *peeled, cored and grated*
1 RED ONION, *grated*
OLIVE OIL, *for frying*

KEFTEDES

This is a slight variation on the classic Greek fried meatballs that all households have. They are light and tasty and probably less fuss to make than you may imagine. Serve them at room temperature, alone or together with other bits and pieces on a meze platter. The Greek and Cypriot meze can really be a mix of anything you like and could be served like an Italian antipasto before a meal, or can sometimes even 'become' the meal, depending on the quantities. Some mezes carry on forever it seems and include meat, fish and a great variety of vegetables and salads.

Break up the bread in a small bowl and add the milk. Leave the bread to soak and absorb the milk, squishing it up so that it dissolves.

Put the meat in a large bowl. Crumble in the mint and add the parsley, eggs, apple, onion and the soaked bread. Season with salt and pepper. Mix through very well with your hands (it will feel quite soft). Roll out small balls about the size of cherry tomatoes, using up all of the mixture. Keep these flat on a tray or board until you're ready to start frying.

Pour 1–2 cm (about ¹/₂ inch) of olive oil into a large non-stick saucepan over medium-high heat. Add a batch of meatballs in a single layer (cook in batches as they will be difficult to turn). Fry until they are golden brown all over, turning carefully with a slotted spoon. Try not to fiddle with them too much as they will be soft and may fall apart.

Remove the cooked meatballs to a plate lined with kitchen paper to absorb the excess oil. They can be served immediately or at room temperature with lemon juice or tzatziki (page 76).

Makes 14

25 g (1 oz) FRESH YEAST
1 TEASPOON SUGAR
500 g (4 cups) BREAD FLOUR
1 TEASPOON SALT
20 g (3/4 oz) BUTTER, *melted*

topping
2 TABLESPOONS OLIVE OIL, *plus extra for drizzling*
1 RED ONION, *chopped*
500 g (1 lb 2 oz) LEAN MINCED (GROUND) LAMB
1/2 TEASPOON GROUND CINNAMON
15 g (1/2 cup) CHOPPED FLAT-LEAF (ITALIAN) PARSLEY
120 g (4 oz) TINNED TOMATOES, *chopped or puréed*
JUICE OF 1 LEMON, *to serve*
CHOPPED CHILLIES IN OIL (SEE OVER), *to serve*

LACHMAJOU

   This is very Middle-Eastern and versatile: like a small pizza, topped with a fairly dry lamb, onion and parsley mixture, baked and then splashed with lemon juice and chilli oil. You could also add a couple of chopped red chillies to the lamb sauté, although I prefer to let people add as much as they like — and my children have it without. This makes 14: you could serve two as a light lunch with a salad; one would do as an antipasto. Or serve them alongside some other Middle-Eastern meze. Ask your butcher to mince the lamb for you or you can do it in the blender. Some people simply mix together the topping ingredients and put this uncooked onto the rolled-out dough that is going to be baked in the oven anyway.

Crumble the yeast into a bowl, sprinkle with the sugar and add 310 ml (1¼ cups) of tepid water. Leave for 10–15 minutes until it begins to activate. Mix in the flour, salt and butter and, when it all comes together, turn out onto a lightly floured work surface and knead well, until the dough is smooth and elastic. Put it back into the bowl and cover with a tea towel, then a heavier towel. Leave in a warm place for about 1½ hours to rise — the dough should puff right up to the top of the bowl.

To make the topping, heat the olive oil in a saucepan and gently sauté the onion to soften it. Add the lamb, cinnamon and most of the parsley. Season with salt and pepper. Cook until any moisture from the lamb has evaporated and the meat is lightly golden, breaking up any clusters with a wooden spoon. Remove from the heat and stir in the tomato. Preheat your oven to 220°C (425°F/Gas 7).

Knock down the dough by punching out all the air to bring it back to its original size. Divide the dough into 14 balls, keeping them covered so they don't dry out. On a lightly floured surface, roll out the dough balls to 1–2 mm thick and about 12–15 cm (5–6 inches) in diameter. Don't worry if they're not completely round: sometimes I make them oval or even a bit triangular. Arrange on lightly floured baking trays and scatter more than a heaped tablespoon of topping over each, leaving a thin border around the edge. Drizzle about a teaspoon of olive oil over each one and bake for a maximum of 10 minutes, or until the dough is just cooked but not dried out. Serve immediately, sprinkled with lemon juice, a little chopped chilli in oil and the rest of the chopped parsley. Cover any that you don't eat with foil. They can be heated quickly in a hot oven or eaten at room temperature.

Makes 1 large jar

ABOUT 40 FRESH RED CHILLIES
SALT
375 ml (1 $^{1}/_{2}$ cups) OLIVE OIL

CHILLIES
IN OLIVE OIL

A teaspoonful of this oil (and a bit of the chilli itself) can be drizzled onto pasta or over grilled (broiled) meats and salads. The oil will initially be very hot, but as it is used you can top it up with more olive oil and it will eventually lose some of its potency. The flavour of the oil will depend entirely on your choice of chillies. Be sure to wear rubber gloves when handling the chillies, as just a little on your skin can prove uncomfortable even a few hours later (especially if you rub your eyes).

Cut the chillies into thin rounds of about 2 mm (about $^{1}/_{16}$ inch). Put them in a colander in the sink and remove as many of the seeds as you can by tapping the colander sharply on the side of the sink. Sprinkle generously with salt and put a plate that fits inside your colander on top of the chillies to squash them and extract some of the juice. Set aside for about 24 hours.

Still using gloves, squeeze the chillies with your hands to drain away the excess salt and moisture and pack them into a clean sterilised jar. Cover them completely with olive oil. The oil will be ready in a couple of days, but will be better in a couple of weeks. Add more olive oil if the chilli oil is too strong. Store in a cool place. The chillies must remain covered by the oil at all times.

Serves 8–10

200 g (7 oz) BURGHUL (BULGAR) WHEAT
1 SMALL RED ONION, *chopped*
1/2 TEASPOON SALT
60 g (2 cups) CHOPPED FLAT-LEAF (ITALIAN)
  PARSLEY
2 TABLESPOONS CHOPPED MINT LEAVES
JUICE OF 2 LEMONS
125 ml (1/2 cup) OLIVE OIL
2 SMALL RIPE TOMATOES, *diced*

TABOULI

You will need to start this salad a few hours, or even a day, before you are going to serve it, as the burghul needs soaking. You can also dress the salad beforehand as the ingredients benefit from some mingling in the bowl. It is just the tomatoes that need to be added not too long before serving, so that they don't become soggy. This is more parsley salad than anything else. I love parsley — I love the idea of eating so much iron.

Put the burghul in a bowl and cover it with about 250 ml (1 cup) cold water. Stir through, cover the bowl with plastic wrap and refrigerate for a few hours or overnight so that the burghul absorbs the water. Stir through a couple of times.

Put the onion in a small bowl, cover with cold water, sprinkle with the salt and leave it for 20 minutes or so before draining away the water and rinsing again.

Drain the burghul through a fine sieve, pushing it gently with a wooden spoon to extract any water. Tip it into a bowl and add the parsley, mint, onion, lemon juice and oil. Season with salt and pepper and mix together well. Keep the salad in the fridge and mix the tomatoes through just before serving.

Makes 25 koupes

shells
115 g (²/₃ cup) FINE BURGHUL (BULGAR) WHEAT OR
  500 g (1 lb 2 oz) FINE BURGHUL (*and no lamb, see below*)
500 g (1 lb 2 oz) LEAN LAMB MINCE
2 RED ONIONS, *chopped*

filling
1 TABLESPOON OLIVE OIL
1 WHITE ONION, *finely chopped*
300 g (10 oz) MINCED (GROUND) PORK AND BEEF
¹/₂ TEASPOON GROUND CINNAMON
30 g (1 oz) PINE NUTS
15 g (¹/₂ cup) CHOPPED PARSLEY
OIL, FOR DEEP-FRYING
LEMONS, *to serve*

KOUPES

These are a wonderful Middle-Eastern speciality. It is good to have a couple of friends helping, as they can be a little tricky, but once you have tasted koupes you will want to know how to make your own. They are shaped like long dumplings or elongated eggs with slightly pointed ends. The outer shell is made with burghul wheat and filled with a mixture of fried mince meat, parsley, cinnamon and pine nuts, then deep-fried. Women who have been making these for a lifetime casually churn out these burghul shells as though they were knitting or doing something quite natural. If you use minced lamb in the shells as well as the burghul, you will find them a lot easier to shape, so I've included both methods.

If you are feeling brave, or have made these before, you can make the shells from just burghul wheat. Put 500 g (1 lb 2 oz) of burghul in a bowl, season with salt and cover with 2¹/₂ cups (625 ml) of just-boiled water. Mix through and, once the wheat has cooled a little, cover the bowl and leave for about 3 hours while you make the filling.

To make the shells by the easier method, put the lamb mince in a food processor and blend to a paste. Transfer to a bowl. Blend the onions to a paste as well, add to the mince and season well with salt and pepper. Mix well and set aside. Rinse the burghul wheat in a sieve under cold running water. Drain well and squeeze out any excess water. Blend in a food processor. Add the mince mixture and blend again. Set aside while you make the filling.

To make the filling, heat the olive oil in a non-stick pan and sauté the onion, stirring, until softened and lightly golden. Add the mince and continue to sauté until all the moisture from the meat has evaporated and it is golden and completely cooked. Break up any clusters with a wooden spoon. Season with salt and pepper and add the cinnamon, stirring constantly to prevent the meat from sticking. Add the pine nuts and cook for another minute or two. Stir in the parsley, then remove from the heat to cool.

Now you are ready to make the shells. Have a small bowl of water ready. If you are using the shell mixture with just burghul, start kneading the burghul wheat in the bowl and then turn it out onto the work surface and knead it as you would a dough (although it will be much harder). It should start to feel softer after a while and then you can break off a chunk about the size of an egg and make it into a ball. If you are using the shell mixture with meat in it, take a ball of the shell mixture about the size of an egg (keep the rest of the mixture covered with a damp cloth to prevent it drying out).

Hold the ball in the cup of your left hand (if you are right-handed). Using your right thumb, flatten the ball so that it takes the shape of your palm, turning upwards like a blanket, and is as thin as you can make it. Add a teaspoonful of the mince mixture and fold the sides of the 'blanket' over the mince. Now you need to seal the top, so, if there is enough shell then do so dipping by your hands lightly in the water and using it like a glue if you find it helps. Or add more shell mixture, pressing it to make uniform, and then cup your hands together, cradling the shell tightly to make it smooth and compact. Put this on a tray while you make the rest.

One-third fill a saucepan or deep-fryer with oil and heat up for deep-frying. Add the koupes a few at a time and deep-fry for 2–3 minutes until dark golden and crisp. Drain on kitchen paper to absorb the excess oil and then serve drizzled with lemon juice and an extra sprinkling of salt. These are also good served at room temperature.

Serves 10

4 TABLESPOONS OLIVE OIL
1 LARGE ONION, *chopped*
2 TABLESPOONS CHOPPED PARSLEY
2 GARLIC CLOVES, *chopped*
850 g (1 lb 14 oz) MINCED (GROUND) PORK AND BEEF
1 BAY LEAF
1 TEASPOON GROUND CINNAMON
125 ml (1/2 cup) WHITE WINE
400 g (14 oz) TINNED TOMATOES, *chopped*
450 g (1 lb) SHORT PASTA
ABOUT 30 g (1 oz) BUTTER
1/2 TEASPOON DRIED MINT
1 TABLESPOON BREADCRUMBS

béchamel sauce
120 g (4 oz) BUTTER
125 g (1 cup) PLAIN (ALL-PURPOSE) FLOUR
1 litre (4 cups) WARM MILK
A LITTLE FRESHLY GRATED NUTMEG

PASTITSIO

I love pastitsio. I have a special glass oval-shaped oven dish that I like to cook it in: it is about 35 cm (14 inches) long, 24 cm (10 inches) wide and 6 cm (2½ inches) deep. Make it in another shaped dish if you like, but it will need to be of similar dimensions (definitely no bigger). It might seem like a lot of fuss and bother, but if you're well organised it can be fun. Pastitsio is best served warm or even at room temperature, with a lovely big Greek salad.

Heat the oil in a large non-stick saucepan and fry the onion until it is soft and lightly golden. Add the parsley and garlic and cook for a few seconds before adding the meat. Fry for a few minutes until all the moisture has evaporated and the mince is starting to brown. Season with salt and pepper and add the bay leaf and cinnamon. When it begins to fry in the oil and brown, add the wine and cook until evaporated. Add the tomatoes and about a cupful of water and continue cooking over medium to low heat for 10–15 minutes until the tomatoes have melted into the meat. The meat shouldn't be too dry. Remove from the heat.

Preheat your oven to 180°C (350°F/Gas 4). Meanwhile, cook the pasta in boiling salted water for 2 minutes less than it says on the packet so that it is still quite firm. Drain and put in a bowl. Mix in the butter and crumble in the mint with your fingers. Mix through well and spoon half over the base of a large ovenproof dish. Pour the meat mixture over the top so it evenly covers the pasta, then add the remaining pasta in another layer over the top. Press down with a wooden spoon so that it is fairly compact. Set aside while you make the béchamel sauce.

Melt the butter in a saucepan. Whisk in the flour and cook for a few minutes, stirring constantly, then begin adding the warm milk. It will be immediately absorbed, so work quickly, whisking with one hand while adding ladlefuls of milk with the other. When the sauce seems to be smooth and not too stiff, add salt, pepper and a grating of nutmeg and continue cooking, even after it comes to the boil, for 5 minutes or so, mixing all the time. It should be a very thick and smooth sauce. Pour this over the pasta and meat layers in the dish. It should just fit exactly in the dish. Sprinkle the breadcrumbs over the top and bake for 30–40 minutes until the top is nicely golden in parts. Let it cool a little before cutting into squares to serve, otherwise it will run everywhere.

My father remembers Yayia making haloumi that was then preserved in salt water with flecks of mint in large clay pots. They would keep them in the loft for the months ahead.

Serves 8

2 LARGE EGGPLANTS (AUBERGINES) (about 1 kg/2 lb 4 oz
    in total)
ABOUT 250 ml (1 cup) LIGHT OLIVE OIL
1 LARGE ONION, *finely chopped*
3 TABLESPOONS ROUGHLY CHOPPED FLAT-LEAF (ITALIAN)
    PARSLEY
2 GARLIC CLOVES, *finely chopped*
850 g (1 lb 14 oz) MINCED (GROUND) PORK AND BEEF
1 TEASPOON GROUND CINNAMON
1/2 TEASPOON DRIED OREGANO
1 BAY LEAF
125 ml (1/2 cup) WHITE WINE
500 g (2 cups) TOMATO PASSATA
500 g (1 lb 2 oz) POTATOES, *peeled*

béchamel sauce
120 g (4 oz) BUTTER
125 g (1 cup) PLAIN (ALL-PURPOSE) FLOUR
1 litre (4 cups) WARM MILK
A LITTLE FRESHLY GRATED NUTMEG

MOUSSAKA

This is more or less how my aunt makes her moussaka. It seems like an incredible job, but you could split up your workload and make the mince sauce the day before (but bring it back to room temperature before putting the moussaka together). If you peel the potatoes in advance, keep them in a bowl of water so that they don't discolour. You could even fry your eggplant and potato a few hours before making the béchamel and putting the moussaka in the oven. The size of the dish is important. I use a transparent oval dish, 35 cm (14 inches) long, 24 cm (10 inches) wide and 6 cm (2 1/2 inches) deep.

Trim the hats off the eggplants, then slice the eggplants lengthways into 5 mm (1/4 inch) slices. Sprinkle salt quite generously over the slices and leave them in the sink or in a bowl for about 30 minutes to draw out any bitter juices.

Heat 3 tablespoons of the oil in a wide non-stick saucepan. Sauté the onion, mixing it with a wooden spoon until it is softened and lightly golden. Add the parsley and garlic and cook for another minute until you can smell the garlic, then add the mince. Cook over medium-high heat until the meat loses its water and begins to brown, shifting it around with a wooden spoon. Add the cinnamon, oregano and bay leaf and season with salt and pepper. When the mince is golden, add the wine and scrape the bottom of the pan with your spoon to make sure no mince is stuck. Let most of the wine evaporate, then add the tomato purée and leave it to simmer for about 30 minutes, uncovered, stirring now and then. Break up any clusters with a wooden spoon. If it seems too dry, add a few more drops of water, but this shouldn't be necessary.

Meanwhile, slice the potatoes lengthways into 5 mm (1/4 inch) slices and pat them dry. Heat 4 or 5 tablespoons of olive oil in a large non-stick saucepan and fry the potatoes in batches over medium heat until they are golden on both sides and cooked through. Remove to a plate lined with kitchen paper, to absorb the oil, and sprinkle with a little salt.

Rinse the salt from the eggplant with cold water and pat dry. Fry in batches in the same pan and oil as the potatoes — they will absorb a lot more oil than the potatoes, so they need a bit of attention. When the underside is golden, turn over and prick with a fork in several places, especially in any still hard bits, so that they are almost collapsing. If you press down with a fork, they should not be hard and papery but instead should be almost like a purée. If they are darkened but not yet soft, stack them on top of the new batch so they can cook for longer. Remove the slices to a plate lined with kitchen paper to absorb some of the oil while you finish the next lot, adding only a tablespoon of oil if possible between batches.

Preheat the oven to 180°C (350°F/Gas 4). Arrange half the eggplant over the base of your oven dish, even slightly overlapping if necessary. Then add the potatoes in a single layer, if possible. Add half the mince, pressing it down with the back of a large spoon. Add the rest of the eggplant in a layer, and then a final layer of mince. Press it down and you should still have about 2½ cm (1 inch) space at the top of the dish.

The béchamel needs to be made just before you bake the moussaka. Melt the butter in a saucepan. Whisk in the flour and cook for a few minutes, stirring constantly, then begin adding the warm milk. It will be immediately absorbed, so work quickly, whisking with one hand while adding ladlefuls of milk with the other. When the sauce seems to be smooth and not too stiff, add salt, pepper and a grating of nutmeg and continue cooking, even after it comes to the boil, for 5 minutes or so, mixing all the time. It should be a very thick and smooth sauce. Taste for seasoning and spoon over the mince. It should come just about flush with the top of the dish.

Bake for 45 minutes – 1 hour with a baking sheet underneath to catch any spills, until the moussaka begins to bubble up and the top is golden in parts. Leave it in the oven to cool slightly before serving. It could even be served at room temperature. Cut into traditional square servings.

YAYIA (my grandmother)
nicosia cyprus

Serves 6

2 RED ONIONS, *roughly chopped*
1.2 kg (2 lb 12 oz) POTATOES, *cut into large chunks*
1 kg (2 lb 4 oz) LAMB, *cut into chunks*
4 TABLESPOONS CHOPPED FLAT-LEAF (ITALIAN)
  PARSLEY
3 HEAPED TEASPOONS CUMIN SEEDS
125 ml (1/2 cup) OLIVE OIL
4 *or* 5 RIPE TOMATOES, *cut into thick slices*
50 g (13/4 oz) BUTTER

TAVA
(CYPRIOT BAKED LAMB & POTATOES
WITH CUMIN & TOMATOES)

This is so simple. It's a very typical Cypriot all-in-one meal — you just need the time to prepare the lamb and vegetables, then you can fling it in the oven, go out for a (Greek) coffee and come home to a ready meal. You could use lamb chops and leave them whole instead of cutting them into chunks, which makes it even simpler. And it doesn't need much by way of accompaniments — perhaps a salad or some simply sautéed vegetables.

Preheat your oven to 180°C (350°F/Gas 4). Put the onion, potato and lamb in a 5 litre- (20 cup-) casserole dish or a deep baking dish. Season with salt and pepper. Add the parsley, cumin and olive oil and mix through very well with your hands. Put the tomato slices on top in a single layer and season lightly with salt. Dot the butter over the top and pour about 125 ml (1/2 cup) of water around the sides of the dish. Cover with foil and bake for 2 hours, tilting the dish from side to side a couple of times and spooning some of the pan juices over the top. The lamb should be very tender and the potatoes soft.

Remove the foil, increase the oven temperature to 200°C (400°F/Gas 6) and cook for another 45 minutes or so, turning the lamb halfway through, or until the meat and potatoes are a little browned and the liquid has reduced. Serve hot or at room temperature.

Serves 4

900 g (2 lb) TARO
100 ml (3¹/₂ fl oz) OLIVE OIL
1 x 1.3 kg (3 lb) CHICKEN, *skinned and cut into 8 serving pieces*
2 RED ONIONS, *chopped*
1 TABLESPOON BUTTER
30 g (1 oz) CELERY LEAVES, *chopped*
2 HEAPED TABLESPOONS TOMATO PASTE (PUREE)
JUICE OF 2 LEMONS

KOLOKASSI

This is a Cypriot dish that we had often during my childhood. It is the taro that gives kolokassi its special flavour, although you could probably make it with another root vegetable like celeriac or even sweet potatoes. This is often made with chunks of pork instead of the chicken — you could use either.

Peel the taro. Don't rinse it, but rub it clean with a damp cloth or kitchen paper. Cut the taro into chunks by just chipping into it with a sharp knife and then breaking off pieces of about 3 cm (an inch). Leave the taro pieces in a bowl with a little splash of lemon juice over them and a sprinkling of salt.

Heat the oil in a wide casserole dish and fry the chicken on both sides until it is lightly golden. Remove the chicken and add the onions to the dish, stirring constantly. When they look like they could start sticking, add the butter and stir for a few minutes more. Return the chicken to the dish, season with salt and pepper and add the celery leaves and taro.

Dissolve the tomato paste in about 3¹/₂ cups (825 ml) of hot water and add to the casserole. When it comes back to the boil, cover, lower the heat to a simmer and cook for about 45 minutes – 1 hour, without stirring the chicken around too much but checking that it doesn't stick. Halfway through this time, add the lemon juice and taste for seasoning.

The chicken and taro should be very tender, but not falling apart, with a good quantity of stewy juice. Leave it to stand for a bit before serving, so that it's not too hot.

Serves 4

1.3 kg (3 lb) BONED SHOULDER OF PORK WITH SOME
    FAT, *cut into slices about 2 cm* (3/4 inch) THICK
500 ml (2 cups) GOOD RED WINE
5 TABLESPOONS OLIVE OIL
2 GARLIC CLOVES, *peeled and squashed a bit*
5 HEAPED TEASPOONS CORIANDER SEEDS, *lightly crushed*
1 *or* 2 BAY LEAVES

AFELIA
(PORK IN RED WINE WITH DRIED CORIANDER SEEDS)

This is a traditional Cypriot dish, so simple and rather wintery with the wonderful, pronounced flavours of dried coriander and good red wine. The pork needs to be marinated ahead of time (24 hours is best, but even a few hours is fine too). Don't crush the coriander seeds too much — they should be almost whole, but pounded just enough to release the magnificently unforgettable flavour. Serve with deep-fried whole new potatoes, cracked wheat (see over), mashed potatoes or a simple white pilaf.

If there is rind on the pork, remove this and any excess fat. Cut the pork into chunks of about 5 cm (2 inches). Put in a bowl with the wine and leave to marinate overnight, or for a few hours in the fridge. Lift out the pork pieces with a slotted spoon (keeping the marinade) and pat dry with kitchen paper.

Heat the oil in a casserole and fry the pork until it is dark golden on all sides. Season with salt and pepper, then add the garlic and coriander. Continue cooking until you can smell the garlic and then add the marinade with the bay leaves and about 1 cup (250 ml) of water. When it begins to boil, lower the heat to a minimum, cover and simmer for about 1½ hours, or until the pork is very tender and there is a fair amount of sauce in the pan. If necessary, add a little more water during cooking. Serve warm.

Place a mince oval onto the centre of each square of caul fat, wrap over from one side, then fold in the edges and roll over on the other side to make a parcel. The caul fat will hold the mixture. Thread onto flat metal skewers (double skewers are a good idea for turning).

Preheat a barbecue or chargrill (griddle) pan to medium hot and barbecue the sheftalia until they are deep golden on all sides, soft inside and completely cooked through. Arrange them on a serving platter and serve with warmed pitta bread and separate bowls of tzatziki, diced tomato, the sliced onion and some lemon wedges.

Pappou would make sausages with coriander seeds and chillies that they would then soak in red wine and put into sausage casings. These were hung up over an outdoor washing line to dry for a few days; he would bring them in at night and take them out again the next morning. They lasted for ages and were eaten grilled over the coals and sliced up on a meze plate. They were also very good fried with eggs for breakfast.

Serves 6 as a side dish

8 LARGE ARTICHOKES (about 200 g/7 oz each)
1 kg (2 lb 4 oz) POTATOES, *peeled*
CORN OIL *or* LIGHT OLIVE, *for deep-frying*
16 SAGE LEAVES, *rinsed and dried*
LEMON WEDGES, *to serve*

FRIED CHIPS &
ARTICHOKE BOTTOMS

This was something special my grandfather made. I added the sage leaves because I am sure that, had he known about their wonderfulness, he would certainly have thrown in a handful at the last moment. Pappou liked to serve his chips in a wide stainless-steel bowl. I remember the way the salt clung to the crispy bits on the side of the bowl that we all fought over. Today I always serve my grandfather's chips in a wide metal bowl.

To prepare the artichokes, rinse them under cold running water and throw away the tough outer leaves. Slice off the stem. Slice the leaves off where they meet the base of the artichoke. (You can slice the leaves thinly, being careful to remove the hairy choke first, then dress with lemon and olive oil and eat as a side salad or scatter over your pizza. They should be kept in lemon water until you dress them.)

Halve the potatoes lengthways. Put them, flat side down, on a chopping board and cut them into chips about 6 mm (1/4 inch) thick. Pat the artichoke bottoms dry with paper towel and cut into three thick slices, like fat chips. (Do this at the last minute, once the potato chips are ready.)

Half-fill a large wide saucepan or deep-fat fryer with oil and heat up for deep-frying. Add the potatoes and give them a stir with a wooden spoon. Leave them for 5 minutes until they look like they are settling and starting to turn golden and soft and then shuffle them around with your wooden spoon so that they actually get a bit mashed up. (These are the bits that will crisp up wonderfully at the end.) Add the artichokes and give a gentle mix, moving the chips from the bottom, and then don't touch them again until they are firm and golden. Now shuffle them again (this should all take about 20 minutes, depending on the heat of your oil). About a minute before you take out the chips, throw in the sage leaves to crisp them up. Lift them all out with a slotted spoon onto a plate lined with kitchen paper and then remove the paper after a couple of minutes. Sprinkle with salt and serve immediately with lemon wedges.

Serves 4–6

1 SMALL ONION, *diced*
1 TEASPOON FINE SALT
2 SMALL TOMATOES, *diced*
A HANDFUL OF CHOPPED PARSLEY
A COUPLE OF LEMONS, *cut into quarters*
300 g (1¹/2 cups) BLACK-EYED BEANS, *soaked overnight*
300 g (10¹/2 oz) ENGLISH SPINACH
EXTRA VIRGIN OLIVE OIL, *to serve*

BLACK-EYED BEANS
WITH
SPINACH

This is probably a mix between a soup and a salad and I like it best when the beans and spinach are still warm. The tomatoes, onion and dressing must all be at room temperature.

Put the onion in a small bowl, cover with cold water and sprinkle with the salt. Leave for about 30 minutes or so. Rinse and drain well, squeezing out the excess water with your hands, and put the onion in a small serving dish. Put the tomatoes, parsley and lemons in separate dishes.

Meanwhile, rinse the beans and put them in a large saucepan. Cover generously with cold water and bring to the boil. Skim any scum from the surface with a slotted spoon. Drain the beans, return to the pan and add fresh water. Bring to the boil again, lower the heat slightly and cook, uncovered, for about 1–1¹/2 hours or until the beans are soft but not mushy. If the water evaporates too quickly, add extra hot water while the beans are cooking — the water level should be just above the beans. Season with salt towards the end of the cooking time. Tear the spinach into bite-sized pieces and add it to the pan. Cook for another 3–5 minutes until the spinach is cooked.

Spoon the beans and spinach into individual bowls with a slotted spoon, adding a trickle of the cooking liquid too. Everyone can dress their own dish with a scattering of parsley, some tomato and onion, salt and pepper, an extra big splash of lemon juice and olive oil.

Serves 4

1 CUCUMBER
2 RIPE TOMATOES, *cut into chunks*
2 INNER CELERY STALKS WITH LEAVES, *chopped*
180 g (6 oz) GREEK OLIVES IN BRINE OR OIL, *drained*
1 SMALL RED ONION, *finely sliced*
40 g ($1^{1}/_{2}$ oz) VALERIANA LEAVES (LAMBS LETTUCE)
A HANDFUL OF CORIANDER (CILANTRO)
1 LARGE GARLIC CLOVE
2 TABLESPOONS GOOD-QUALITY RED WINE
  VINEGAR
125 ml ($^{1}/_{2}$ cup) OLIVE OIL
150 g ($5^{1}/_{2}$ oz) FETA CHEESE, *roughly crumbled*
1 TEASPOON DRIED OREGANO

GREEK-CYPRIOT SALAD

This is more or less how my grandfather would make a salad and serve it, in a big bowl, ready dressed for everyone to help themselves. Use lemon juice instead of vinegar if you like, and you could add other ingredients to these.

Peel away the skin of the cucumber in alternate stripes lengthways. Halve lengthways and then cut into slices and put in your serving bowl.

Add the tomatoes, celery, olives, onion, lettuce and coriander to the bowl. Season with salt and pepper and mix through.

Mix the garlic and vinegar with a pinch of salt in a blender until completely smooth. Stir in the oil. Pour over the salad and gently mix through, adding more salt (but remembering that the feta may be quite salty) or pepper if necessary. Crumble the feta and oregano over the top before serving.

Makes about 35 puffs

20 g (3/4 oz) FRESH YEAST
200 g (1²/3 cups) PLAIN (ALL-PURPOSE) FLOUR
¹/2 TEASPOON SUGAR
A PINCH OF SALT
400 g (14 oz) POTATOES
175 g (¹/2 cup) RUNNY HONEY
JUICE OF HALF A LEMON
¹/2 TEASPOON GROUND CINNAMON
LIGHT OIL, *for deep-frying*

LOUKOUMADES
(DEEP-FRIED HONEY &
CINNAMON SYRUP PUFFS)

I remember eating these in the summer cool of the Cyprus mountains. They are quite rich and probably just two per person is the best quantity — served with a glass of iced water or a coffee as an afternoon treat, rather than a dessert. You might not need to make so many at once, but you can easily halve the amounts. There are places in Greece and Cyprus (and probably else-where) that specialise in these. I imagine they keep their batter in the fridge to slow down the yeast process and fry a few at a time as needed, then shower them from a large pot of communal syrup.

Crumble the yeast into a large bowl. Add 375 ml (1¹/2 cups) of warm water with a handful of the flour, the sugar and salt and stir through. Cover and leave for about 30 minutes in a warm place until the yeast begins to activate. Meanwhile, peel and rinse the potatoes, then boil until soft. Mash them well.

Add the rest of the flour to the yeast bowl, along with the potatoes. Whisk well until you have a smooth, loose batter. Cover the bowl and leave again for 1¹/2–2 hours in a warm place, or until the batter looks a bit frothy on the surface and has puffed up and is quite thick (otherwise the puffs will collapse when you fry them).

To make the syrup, put the honey, lemon juice and cinnamon in a saucepan with about 3 tablespoons of water and boil for 10 minutes until thickened. Remove from the heat.

Put enough oil in a wide saucepan to come about 4 cm (1¹/2 inches) up the side and heat up for deep-frying. Take teaspoonfuls of the batter and push gently into the hot oil with a second teaspoon. Fry for a minute or so, just until they have puffed up, are lightly golden on all sides and cooked through. Reduce the temperature if it seems the outsides are browning too quickly and the insides remaining uncooked. Drain on kitchen paper and then transfer to a serving bowl. Pour the warm syrup over the fried puffs and serve hot.

_ Cyprus _

Serves 10

250 g (1¹/4 cups) LONG- *or* MEDIUM-GRAIN RICE
2 litres (8 cups) MILK
3 TABLESPOONS SUGAR
GROUND CINNAMON (or a little rose water), *to serve*

RICE
PUDDING

This is my grandfather through and through. When I asked for recipes he would give me vague measures: 'Add one flat woodenspoonful of sugar and cook it until it is ready'. I remember him always in his work shed, stirring away at this on the gas stove. He liked to sometimes splash in some rose water, but more often just scattered a little ground cinnamon over the crust-formed top. We always liked to eat one just-made warm and have another cold from the fridge for breakfast the next morning. You can add a little more sugar if you prefer your rice pudding sweeter.

Put the rice in a heavy-based saucepan, cover generously with water and bring to the boil. Boil for 20 minutes, then thoroughly drain the rice. Rinse out the pan and pour in the milk. When it comes to a rolling boil, add the rice and bring it back to the boil. Lower the heat and simmer for 20 minutes, stirring often with a wooden spoon to make sure it doesn't stick. Stir in the sugar and simmer for 10 minutes more before removing from the heat. Leave to cool for about 15 minutes in the pan, then spoon out, making sure you get some of the thickened liquid and rice in each portion. Sprinkle with ground cinnamon before serving. This can be eaten immediately or put in the fridge for a few hours.

Pappou was quiet; he had integrity and no flashness about him. He always wore a perfectly ironed shirt, gilet in winter, polished shoes and had his hair slicked back with the special cream he ordered from Italy. He never demanded acknowledgement, but dashed around quietly with the energy of milk just at that rolling boil.

PAPPOU (my grandfather)
nicosia cyprus

Serves 4

poached pears
160 g (²/₃ cup) CASTER (SUPERFINE) SUGAR
10 cm (4 inch) PIECE LEMON PEEL, *pith removed*
1 CINNAMON STICK
4 SMALL RIPE BUT FIRM PEARS, *peeled, halved and cored*
2 BEAUTIFUL UNTREATED ROSES, *petals removed and rinsed*

filo pastry
3 SHEETS (50 x 37 cm/20 x 15 inch) FILO PASTRY
50 g (13/4 oz) BUTTER, *melted*
30 g (1 oz) CASTER (SUPERFINE) SUGAR
3 TABLESPOONS MILD-FLAVOURED RUNNY HONEY

praline
3 TABLESPOONS CASTER (SUPERFINE) SUGAR
30 g (¹/₄ cup) UNSALTED SHELLED PISTACHIO NUTS
4 SCOOPS VANILLA ICE CREAM
ICING (CONFECTIONERS') SUGAR, *to serve*

FILO WITH POACHED PEARS
& ROSE PETALS, PISTACHIO PRALINE
& VANILLA ICE CREAM

This is my personal variation on a baklava; I love the way it looks. You can change or adapt the recipe — leave out the praline, serve pistachio or cinnamon ice cream instead, or biscuits instead of the filo if you want to simplify it. You could also poach plums or peaches instead of the pears. The filo can be baked beforehand (if it loses its crispness, just put it back in a hot oven for a couple of minutes). You'll probably serve just one pear half per person so keep the rest in the fridge in their syrup for the next day.

To make the poached pears, put the sugar, lemon peel, cinnamon stick and about 500 ml (2 cups) of water in a fairly wide saucepan and bring to the boil. Boil for 5 minutes, then add the pears. Lower the heat to minimum so that it doesn't bubble up. Lay a piece of baking paper directly onto the pears and liquid to prevent the exposed part of the pears from discolouring. Simmer for 10–15 minutes, until the pears look slightly transparent and are soft but not falling apart (the cooking time will depend on their size and ripeness). Add the rose petals, keeping a small handful back, and simmer for another couple of minutes. Remove the pan from the heat and leave to cool.

Preheat your oven to 180°C (350°F/Gas 4) and either grease a baking tray or line it with baking paper. Put one sheet of filo pastry on the work surface and brush liberally with the melted butter. Scatter half the sugar over the pastry with gentle flicking wrist movements and then cover with a second sheet of filo. Repeat the butter and sugar technique and then add the last sheet of filo, brushing the top with butter. You will have to work quite quickly and, if it is the first time you are using filo pastry, you might like to have an assistant. Halve the pastry lengthways and then, using a ruler and a sharp knife, cut 9 lines down at 5 cm (2 inch) intervals so that you have 20 strips. Put the strips on the baking tray. Drizzle each one with a little honey and bake for 10–15 minutes, or until golden and crisp. Transfer them to a tray lined with clean baking paper (or else they will stick), leave to cool and then store open, covered with a layer of baking paper. Handle gently as they are delicate.

Butter or oil a flat baking tray. To make the praline, put the sugar in a small saucepan over medium heat. Leave to melt for about 4 minutes, until it turns to caramel — don't stir, but you can swirl the pan around a couple of times. Remove the caramel from the heat, taking care that it doesn't burn, and stir in the nuts. Pour onto the tray and then leave until cold and set. Break up the pieces, then bash with a heavy mallet or pulse in a food processor until the praline is in coarse crumbs.

To serve, put one or two pear halves with the rose petals and a little syrup in a bowl. Add a scoop of ice cream, then two or three filo strips. Scatter with some praline, sprinkle with icing sugar and your extra rose petals and serve immediately.

Always, always upon arrival in Cyprus I would find a box of my favourite baklava, ribboned and waiting for me. Pure chance, his expression seemed to say when I looked at him questioningly. Pappou never said much, but I could tell he loved us all sitting under the lemon tree, late into the summer night, while the crickets carried on and on with their chanting.

Serves 20

125 g (4^1/$_2$ oz) BUTTER, *softened*
230 g (1 cup) CASTER (SUPERFINE) SUGAR
250 g (1 cup) PLAIN YOGHURT (NOT TOO THICK OR THIN)
1 TABLESPOON ROSE WATER
3 EGGS, *separated*
^{1}/$_2$ TEASPOON GRATED LIME RIND
125 g (1 cup) PLAIN (ALL-PURPOSE) FLOUR
125 g (1 cup) FINE SEMOLINA
2 TEASPOONS BAKING POWDER
55 g (^{1}/$_2$ cup) GROUND ALMONDS

rose water syrup
230 g (1 cup) CASTER (SUPERFINE) SUGAR
1 TEASPOON ROSE WATER

YOGHURT & SEMOLINA SYRUP CAKE WITH ROSE WATER

This is a very typical, and very sweet, Cypriot cake. You can leave out the rose water and make a plain syrup-drenched cake, or add lemon juice, vanilla extract or orange blossom water to the syrup.

Preheat your oven to 180°C (350°F/Gas 4). Grease and flour a 22 cm (9 inch) square cake tin. Cream the butter and sugar together in a large bowl with electric beaters. Whisk in the yoghurt, rose water, egg yolks and lime rind. Sift in the flour, semolina and baking powder and mix well to incorporate. Mix in the ground almonds. In a separate bowl, whisk the egg whites until they are white, fluffy and just making soft peaks. Carefully fold these into the mixture so that they are well incorporated. Pour the batter into the tin and bake for about 45 minutes, or until the cake is deep golden and cooked through. Leave to cool while making the syrup.

To make the syrup, put the sugar, rose water and 250 ml (1 cup) of water in a small saucepan and boil for about 5 minutes. Pour the hot syrup over the cake and leave it to cool completely. To serve, cut the cake into small pieces and serve with a not-too-sweet ice cream (such as the mastika ice cream overleaf).

Serves 8

1 FLAT TEASPOON MASTIKA GRANULES
200 g (7 oz) CASTER (SUPERFINE) SUGAR
500 ml (2 cups) MILK
500 ml (2 cups) POURING (SINGLE) CREAM

MASTIKA
ICE CREAM

This has such a definite flavour (you might recognise it from Turkish delight). I love it on its own, or served alongside a sweet dessert such as the yoghurt cake with rose water. I have a friend in Cyprus who always chews mastika, which she buys in small flat squares, instead of chewing gum. It is unscented and unsweetened; if you are serving it on its own you could add some other flavourings such as a few drops of rose water or a liqueur. Mastika is sold in crystals and I use a small coffee or spice-grinder to make it into a powder. It gives the ice cream a wonderful, almost chewy, texture and is good when you want a slightly less sweet accompaniment.

Put the mastika with a teaspoon or so of the sugar into a small grinder and grind to a fine powder. Heat the milk with the remaining sugar and ground mastika, stirring (or whisking) until it comes to the boil, so that it has completely dissolved. Remove from the heat. Let it cool a bit, whisking now and then, and then mix in the cream. Transfer to a bowl, cover and put in the freezer.

After an hour, remove the bowl from the freezer, give an energetic whisk with a hand whisk or electric mixer and return the bowl to the freezer. Whisk again after another couple of hours. When it is nearly firm, give one last whisk, transfer to a suitable freezing container with a lid and let it set in the freezer until it is firm.

Alternatively, pour the mixture into your ice-cream machine and freeze, following the manufacturer's instructions.

preserved orange peel
10 ORANGES (ABOUT 2 KG/4 LB 8 OZ)
375 g (1²/₃ cups) CASTER (SUPERFINE) SUGAR

preserved cherries
1 kg (2 lb 4 oz) CHERRIES
300 g (10¹/₂ oz) CASTER (SUPERFINE) SUGAR
JUICE OF 1 LEMON

preserved green plums
1 kg (2 lb 4 oz) SMALL GREEN PLUMS
300 g (10¹/₂ oz) CASTER (SUPERFINE) SUGAR
1 LONG STRIP ORANGE RIND, PLUS THE JUICE OF
   1 ORANGE
1 BAY LEAF

figs in syrup
500 g (1 lb 2 oz) NATURALLY DRIED FIGS *or* 1 kg
   (2 lb 4 oz) FRESH FIGS
500 g (1 lb 2 oz) CASTER (SUPERFINE) SUGAR
JUICE OF 1 LEMON
1 VANILLA BEAN, *cut in half lengthways*
1 TABLESPOON RUM *or* BRANDY

PRESERVED FRUITS
IN SUGAR SYRUP

These are something that many Cypriot and Greek people have in their fridge and offer to visitors with a glass of ice-cold water or a coffee. They are eaten straight off the spoon and some people like to then stir their syrupy spoon into their glass of water. You can preserve almost any small fruits with this recipe: baby clementines, tiny eggplants (aubergines), green walnuts, bergamo or figs and keep them in the fridge. These are normally extremely sweet — I have used slightly less sugar but you can add more if you prefer.

PRESERVED ORANGE PEEL

Rinse the oranges in warm water. Peel off the skin with a good potato peeler, trying not to press too hard so that you leave behind the white pith and remove only the outer orange peel. Do this lengthways or around the circumference, whichever way works best for you. If lengthways, you should get six or seven strips. Around the circumference you should get about three long strips: halve these so you have pieces about 9 cm (3¹/₂ inches) long. If there is a lot of pith on the strips, put them on a wooden board, pith side up, and run a small sharp knife along each strip to remove the white pith. You should be left with about 200 g (7 oz) of peel.

Boil the orange peel in water for about 15 minutes until softened, then drain. Roll up each piece of peel fairly tightly and thread onto a length of cotton with a needle, as if you were stringing a necklace together (this will help the peel hold its shape in the syrup).

Put the sugar in a saucepan with 450 ml (16 fl oz) water and the juice of one of the oranges and bring to the boil. Lower to a simmer, drop in the orange peel necklace and cover the surface with a piece of baking paper to hold the peel in the syrup. Simmer gently for about 45 minutes, then remove the peel and take it off the thread. Put the peel in a suitable preserving jar.

The syrup should have thickened during cooking, if not cook it for slightly longer. Pour the syrup over the peel (it should just cover it). When cool, refrigerate, ensuring the peel is covered by the syrup, and use within a month.

PRESERVED CHERRIES

Pit the cherries carefully with a thin pitter and then rinse them. Put the sugar, lemon juice and 250 ml (1 cup) water in a saucepan and bring to the boil. Add the cherries and, when they come to the boil, cover with a piece of greaseproof paper to keep them submerged. Simmer gently for 6–8 minutes, turning them now and then to make sure they are covered. Remove the pan from the heat (the cherries must not be too soft). Using a slotted spoon, spoon the cherries into a suitable preserving jar.

Continue boiling the syrup for about 10 minutes or until it has reduced by half. Strain through muslin over the cherries and seal the jar when cool. The cherries should always be covered by syrup. These are normally served straight from the fridge, with a spoon and small plate and a glass of iced water to cut through their beautiful over-sweetness. Use within a month.

PRESERVED GREEN PLUMS

The green plums look nice served whole, so leave the stones in and spit them out as you go. If you would prefer them to be pitted beforehand, make a small slit and remove the stone.

Rinse the plums. Put the sugar, orange rind, juice and bay leaf in a saucepan with about 1 litre (4 cups) of water and bring to the boil. Add the plums and, when the syrup comes back to the boil, lower the heat and cover with a piece of greaseproof paper to keep the plums submerged. Simmer gently for 8–10 minutes, turning them now and then to make sure they are all covered.

Remove from the heat (the plums must not be too soft). Using a slotted spoon, spoon the plums into a suitable preserving jar. Leave the syrup to boil for about 12–15 minutes until it has reduced by about two-thirds. Pour over the plums and seal when cool. The plums should always be covered by syrup. Keep in the fridge and use within a month.

FIGS IN SYRUP

If you are using dried figs, soak them in warm water for at least a couple of hours, then drain.

Put the sugar, lemon juice, vanilla bean and 625 ml (2½ cups) water in a saucepan and bring to the boil over medium heat. Add the figs, lower the heat and cook, uncovered, for about 20 minutes. Remove the softened figs with a slotted spoon to a plate. If your syrup is still very watery and pale, boil it until it has thickened a little.

Put the figs into a suitable preserving jar. Let the syrup cool and then pour it over the figs in the jar. Pour the rum or brandy over the top. Top with a circle of greaseproof paper (or a preserving paper disc), pushing down on the figs to keep them submerged in the syrup, and seal the jars tightly. Once opened, store in the fridge and use within a month. These are particularly delicious served with thick cream.

Pappou's orange tree

Pappou used to climb up the ladder propped against his orange tree and twist off the oranges that my grandmother would later preserve with sugar syrup. My father remembers them all sitting there — Yayia, Aunty Annou and a couple of others — threading the orange necklaces.

Serves 12

sponge
3 EGGS
115 g (¹/₂ cup) CASTER (SUPERFINE) SUGAR
140 g (5 oz) PLAIN (ALL-PURPOSE) FLOUR
A PINCH OF SALT
1 TEASPOON VANILLA EXTRACT

100 g (3¹/₂ oz) ALMONDS
2 LITRES (8 cups) MILK, *plus* 4 TABLESPOONS
1 LARGE EGG
70 g (2¹/₂ oz) CASTER (SUPERFINE) SUGAR
110 g (4 oz) CORNFLOUR (CORNSTARCH)
3 TABLESPOONS ROSE WATER
3 TABLESPOONS COGNAC
380 g (13 oz) PRESERVED FRUITS IN SUGAR SYRUP (draine
  weight), *cut into chunks, plus some syrup* (SEE PAGE 201)

CHARLOTTA
(CYPRIOT TRIFLE WITH ROSE WATER & PRESERVED FRUITS)

This is my father's favourite dessert; it reminds him of his childhood. Charlotta is a dessert that many Cypriot children have grown up with — a Middle-Eastern flavoured trifle, which is good to serve after a meal that has even a hint of those Middle-Eastern spices. Between the two layers of sponge are pieces of special fruit in their sweet syrup, a splashing of brandy and rose water, and a layer of pastry cream. Try your hardest to get hold of green (unripe) walnuts in syrup — they seem an essential special taste in this dessert. If not, choose your favourite fruits in syrup, either bought or home-made. I like to make this in that same oval glass dish that my grandmother always used.

Preheat the oven to 180°C (350°F/Gas 4). Butter and flour a 35 x 24 cm (14 x 10 inch) dish. To make the sponge, whip the eggs and the sugar for about 10 minutes with electric beaters on high speed until they are very, very thick and creamy and have bulked up a lot. Add the sifted flour, the salt and vanilla and fold in gently. Scrape out every drop into your dish, swinging the dish from side to side so that the batter goes to the edges evenly. Bake for about 20 minutes, or until the top is golden brown and the cake is cooked through and feels spongy. Turn out the sponge onto a wooden board to cool, and halve it horizontally through the middle with a long bread knife. Set aside for now and wash the dish.

GEORGE in his youth
nicosia cyprus

Put the almonds in a blender and pulse-chop for a bit until they are coarse chunks. Remove about 4 tablespoons of the coarser chunks and continue pulsing the rest until they are finely chopped. Lightly toast the 4 tablespoons of coarser nuts under the grill (broiler) or in a dry frying pan until they are lightly golden. Set aside for now.

Meanwhile, make the cream. Put most of the 2 litres (8 cups) of milk in a saucepan, keeping about half a cupful on one side, and bring just to the boil, them remove it from the heat for now. Whisk together the egg and sugar with electric beaters until fluffy. Put the half a cup of cold milk in a bowl and gradually add the cornflour, stirring until it is smooth and dissolved. Whisk the dissolved cornflour into the egg mix. Add a ladleful of the hot milk to the egg mixture, whisking quickly to prevent any curdling, and then add another ladleful. Incorporate all the egg mixture into the milk pan and put it back over gentle heat, whisking all the time, until it starts to thicken and make bubbles on the surface. The whisk will start to leave thick trails behind it, so let it bubble for a few minutes and then remove the pan from the heat. Stir in a tablespoon of rose water and the finely chopped almonds. Leave to cool a bit, whisking now and then. (The cream should look like a very pale, fairly loose custard and will thicken more as it cools, and then later in the fridge.)

Put one layer of sponge back into the clean glass dish. In a cup, mix together the 4 tablespoons of milk, the rose water and Cognac and dribble (or brush) about half of this evenly over the sponge layer. Cut up about four pieces of fruit in syrup and arrange these over the sponge. Drizzle about 2 tablespoons of the thick fruit syrup over the sponge, and then pour over about half of the cooled cream, spreading it gently to cover the sponge completely.

Put the second layer of sponge on top. Drizzle the rest of the milk, rose water and Cognac mixture over the sponge, scatter with another four pieces of chopped fruit and drizzle with 2 more tablespoons of syrup. Finally spread the rest of the cream over the sponge, so that it is almost flush with the top of the dish. Scatter with the toasted almonds and leave to cool. Once cooled, cover the dish and put into the fridge. Leave it for at least a couple of hours before serving.

Yayia's red sweets

The sweets from Yayia, my grandmother, were perfect square treasures, wrapped up in red. I can definitely remember their taste, even though I was so small. They weren't rose, although my grandparents would use rose or lemon blossom water in their desserts.

— Cyprus —

Serves 4

80 g (2³/4 oz) RICE FLOUR
90 g (¹/3 cup) CASTER (SUPERFINE) SUGAR
1 TEASPOON ROSE WATER
550 ml (19 fl oz) MILK

rose water syrup
80 g (2³/4 oz) CASTER (SUPERFINE) SUGAR
60 ml (¹/4 cup) HOT WATER
2 TEASPOONS ROSE WATER
185 ml (3/4 cup) ICED WATER

MAHALEPI

Mahalepi always makes me think of Cyprus, jasmine and those hot, hot summers. It is light, milky and Middle-Eastern tasting and always beautifully refreshing after a spicy meal. It is a taste you have to get used to but I know many people who are crazy about mahalepi.

Put the flour, sugar, rose water, milk and 550 ml (19 fl oz) water in a saucepan and bring to the boil, whisking constantly. Continue whisking for a couple of minutes and then remove from the heat. Leave to cool slightly, then pour into four serving dishes. Cool completely, then put in the fridge.

Now make the rose water syrup. Dissolve the sugar in the hot water with the rose water, then leave to cool. Add the iced water (even with a few ice cubes) and put the syrup in the fridge to get very cold.

To serve, drizzle a few spoonfuls of syrup over each dish at the last moment. If you want to colour the syrup, add a few red rose petals or cherries.

Makes 24

pastry
250 g (9 oz) CAKE FLOUR *or* PLAIN (ALL-PURPOSE)
    FLOUR
70 g (2¹/2 oz) COLD BUTTER, *diced*
FINELY GRATED RIND OF 1 SMALL LEMON

filling
200 g (7 oz) RICOTTA *or* SMOOTH CREAM CHEESE
¹/2 TEASPOON GROUND CINNAMON
¹/2 TEASPOON ORANGE BLOSSOM WATER
25 g (1 oz) CASTER (SUPERFINE) SUGAR

LIGHT OLIVE OIL., *for deep-frying*
ICING (CONFECTIONERS') SUGAR, *to serve*

BOUREKIA
(DEEP-FRIED CREAM CHEESE &
CINNAMON PASTRIES)

These are normally made with anari cheese, but you can use ricotta or a smooth cream cheese or something else similar. These deep-fried pastries are scattered with icing sugar and are best eaten warm.

To make the pastry, put the flour and butter in a large bowl with a pinch of salt. Mix in, sifting and working it through your fingers until it forms large crumbs. Add 5 tablespoons water and the lemon rind and knead gently and quickly with your hands until the dough just comes together in a mass. Knead for 20–30 seconds or until smooth. Take care not to overwork the dough. Wrap in plastic wrap and leave for about 1 hour in a cool (but not cold) place.

To make the filling, mix the ricotta or cream cheese with the cinnamon, orange blossom water and caster sugar. Refrigerate until needed.

Roll out the pastry very thinly. Cut rounds of about 8 cm (3 inches), using a biscuit cutter or sharp-rimmed glass. Put a teaspoon of the filling in the middle of each round. Wet your finger with a little water and run it around the edge of the pastry, then fold it over into a half moon. Press the edge to make sure it is sealed.

Keep all the pastries on a tray dusted with flour until you are ready to fry them. Fill a saucepan or deep-fat fryer one-third full of oil and heat up for deep-frying. Fry the pastries a few at a time for 30–40 seconds, turning them around until they are golden. Lift them out with tongs onto a tray lined with kitchen paper to drain off the oil. Arrange on a serving plate, dust very generously with icing sugar and serve immediately.

Makes 625 ml (2¹/₂ cups) jam and 4 puddings

jam
1 kg (2 lb 4 oz) RIPE WATERMELON FLESH (about
    1.8 kg/4 lb watermelon with peel)
400 g (1³/4 cups) CASTER (SUPERFINE) SUGAR
1 LEMON
1 GORGEOUS UNTREATED ROSE, *petals separated
    and rinsed*

buttermilk pudding
4 GELATINE LEAVES (less than 2 g each) *or*
    2 TEASPOONS GELATINE POWDER
250 ml (1 cup) CREAM
100 g (3¹/2 oz) CASTER (SUPERFINE) SUGAR
A FEW DROPS OF VANILLA EXTRACT
450 ml (16 fl oz) BUTTERMILK

WATERMELON &
ROSE PETAL JAM WITH BUTTERMILK
PUDDING

As far as I am concerned, roses in food are the epitome of gorgeous.
If you want to make this jam more rosy, add a few drops of rose water, and
if you have any petals left over you can always scatter them in your bath.
This jam is quite runny and has a beautiful colour — it would be wonderful
dribbled over a not-too-sweet ice cream or served with a blob of crème
fraiche. If you can manage it, make the jam with the first of the watermelons
and the last of the roses. If you prefer your jam thicker, cook half a chopped
apple with the watermelon. You may need more or less sugar, depending on
the sweetness of your watermelon. The buttermilk pudding would also be
lovely served with some other fruit — perhaps syrupy poached quinces or a
mixed berry salad. I like to use smooth pudding saucepans here, but you can
use any ramekins you like. You can even serve the pudding in its ramekin with
a little bowl of jam on the side.

To make the jam, put the watermelon in a bowl and sprinkle with the sugar. Halve the lemon
and cut 3 thin slices from one half. Cut these slices into 8 pieces each and add to the bowl.
Juice the remaining lemon and add to the bowl. Cover with plastic wrap and leave in the
fridge overnight.

Pour the sugary fruit into a heavy-based saucepan suitable for making jam and bring to the boil. Lower the heat and simmer uncovered for about 1 hour, stirring frequently with a wooden spoon so that it doesn't stick. Ten minutes or so before you think it will be ready, remove half of the jam to a blender (making sure there are no lemon pieces included because those are nice left whole) and leave the rest of the jam to continue cooking. Purée this half and return it to the pan. (A few bits of watermelon and lemon give the jam a nice texture.)

To test if your jam is ready, spoon a little onto a plate and tilt it. It should slide down with resistance rather than just running down. If necessary, cook for longer. Add the rose petals and pour into a suitable sterilised jar, using a wide-necked funnel if necessary. Seal the jar tightly and turn over. Leave it to cool completely before turning the jar upright and storing in a cool place. Once opened, keep in the refrigerator and use up fairly quickly.

To make the puddings, soak the gelatine leaves in a bowl with enough cold water to cover them (you can snap the leaves of gelatine). If using powder, put 2 tablespoons of water in a glass bowl and sprinkle the gelatine evenly over the top. Leave to sponge and swell.

Put the cream, sugar and vanilla in a saucepan over medium heat to dissolve the sugar, then remove from the heat. Thoroughly squeeze out the softened gelatine leaves with your hands until they are like a ball of jelly. Add the gelatine leaves or the spongy gelatine to the warm cream and stir to dissolve it. Leave the mixture to cool, stirring from time to time to ensure the gelatine dissolves evenly. When completely cooled, stir in the buttermilk and strain through a sieve to remove any lumps of gelatine. Ladle into four 175 ml (2/3 cup) capacity ramekins. Put these on a tray, cover lightly with plastic wrap and put them in the fridge for at least a couple of hours before serving.

To serve, gently loosen around the sides of the puddings with your fingers or the back of a teaspoon. Dip the bottoms of the ramekins in a little hot water for a couple of seconds (no longer, or you'll end up with soup) and turn them out. Or, simply scoop out with a large spoon and pour some jam over the top before serving.

_ Cyprus _

MONKEYS' WEDDINGS

South Africa

MONKEYS' WEDDINGS

On Saturday afternoons we often had picnics on the flat mossy rocks that served as tables in the river at the bottom of our road. On Sundays we liked to pack our barbecue in the car and drive to a small waterfall where we would spend our day. This was before we had a garden and we would make barbecued mushrooms, brushing them with lemon, garlic and olive oil as they cooked. We passed the black ladies in the river on the way, undressed and grating their clothes on the rocks, sloshing away at them with their feet. It was our very favourite spectacle.

From our windows at home we watched boys on bicycles with large sacks of pale long-husked corn, and tore out to buy a couple that would later drip warmly with butter. The sad music from those old white ice-cream vans selling soft-serve would pierce deep into our homes, so that we could run outside with our coins stuffed into our palms.

We liked to sit on the floor with our nanny, in the safety of her big arms, eating with our hands, clumping the soft maizemeal between our fingers and dipping this into the sauce from the meat stew (our nanny loved her meat burnt).

We loved swimming at night. And there were those storms that thrilled us but drove my mother under the bed covers, terrified, waiting for the thunder and lightning to pass. They never had those kinds of storms in Finland.

It is the smell of those moments before an African summer thunderstorm that remains with me, and the swims afterwards as we looked for the rainbow and tried to guess the exact point where the monkeys' wedding was happening.

There is something about the African landscape, the bush and the night sky, that covers me with silence. And those baobab trees that witness all and still stay in standing ovation to the magnificence of such a land.

Serves 6–8

8 LARGE GARLIC CLOVES
150 g (5¹/2 oz) BUTTER, *softened*
2 TABLESPOONS CHOPPED PARSLEY
1 LONG BAGUETTE

GARLIC
BREAD

This takes me back many years to one of my favourite restaurants in South Africa. It was a standard everywhere, I think — a good rack of ribs, this bread and then tiny scoops of vanilla ice cream that had been dipped in chocolate. This quantity will make a generous amount of garlic butter, but you can press any leftover into a long roll in baking paper, twist the sides like a large sweet wrapper and freeze it. Cut off slices to serve with your pan-fried fillet steaks, barbecued sirloin steaks or pan-fried chicken breasts.

Preheat the oven to 180°C (350°F/Gas 4). Chop the garlic very finely, then add a little salt and squash it with the flat of the knife until it is almost a purée. Mix very thoroughly with the butter and parsley.

Cut the baguette in half to make it more manageable. Slice the baguette slightly on the diagonal, without cutting all the way through. Using a teaspoon, spread some butter into each cavity, taking care that the slices don't break off and separate from the loaf. Both sides should be generously buttered.

Wrap the baguette in foil and bake for 20 minutes or so, until the garlic butter has melted completely and the bread is quite crispy. If the bread seems soft, you can open the foil for a few minutes to crisp it up, depending on the type of bread you use. Serve immediately.

(If you don't want to eat the bread immediately, wrap it in foil before baking and keep it in the freezer. When ready to serve, put it straight from the freezer into the hot oven and bake it for a little longer than specified.)

Makes 1 loaf

1 SMALL POTATO
25 g (1 oz) FRESH YEAST
60 ml (¹/4 cup) BEER, *at room temperature*
¹/2 TEASPOON CASTER (SUPERFINE) SUGAR
4 TABLESPOONS CORN *or* SUNFLOWER SEED OIL
350 g (12 oz) KAMUT FLOUR, *or* SPELT FLOUR
100 g (3¹/2 oz) BREAD FLOUR (*or 200 g/7 oz if you are using spelt*)
1 TEASPOON SALT

KAMUT
BREAD

This is something that I first tasted in South Africa, although it is of Egyptian origin. Kamut is a grain whose taste I love; you could even use all kamut flour and leave out the little bit of white bread flour used in this recipe. Kamut is available in health food shops, but if you can't find it you can use the spelt flour instead. This quantity makes enough for two small loaves or one larger one, and the bread freezes well.

Boil the potato until it is soft, then drain and peel it. Crumble the yeast into a small bowl and add the beer, sugar, oil and 1 cup (250 ml) of tepid water. Leave for 10 minutes or so, until it begins to activate.

Put the flours in a larger bowl with the salt. Mash up the potato and add it to the flour. Mix in the yeast mixture, first with a wooden spoon and then with your hands when it becomes too thick. Knead for about 10 minutes on your work surface until you have a soft dough. Sprinkle a little white flour onto your work surface to prevent it from sticking, if necessary — the consistency should improve as you knead it.

Put the dough back in the bowl and cover with a clean towel, then with a heavier towel. Leave to rise for 1¹/2–2 hours until it has puffed up well.

Preheat the oven to 220°C (425 F/Gas 7). Knock back the dough by punching out all the air to bring it back to its original size. Knead for a minute or so and form it into a ball about 20 cm (8 inches) in diameter. Line a baking tray with baking paper and put the bread on the tray. Dust lightly with flour, cover loosely with a tea towel and leave in a warm place (next to your heating oven) for another 20–30 minutes to rise.

Remove the cloth and bake for about 30 minutes or until the bread is nicely golden and the crust feels firm. Cool slightly before slicing.

Serves 3–4

dipping sauce
100 g (3½ oz) FIRM BLUE CHEESE
250 g (1 cup) PLAIN YOGHURT (not too thick)
1 TABLESPOON LEMON JUICE
1 GARLIC CLOVE, *very finely chopped*
1 TABLESPOON OLIVE OIL

sauce for coating wings
85 g (3 oz) BUTTER
1 TABLESPOON APPLE CIDER VINEGAR *or* WHITE WINE
   VINEGAR
2 TEASPOONS TABASCO *or* OTHER HOT SAUCE
½ TEASPOON SWEET PAPRIKA

6 CHICKEN WINGS
PLAIN (ALL-PURPOSE) FLOUR, *for dusting*
VEGETABLE *or* LIGHT OLIVE OIL, *for frying*
ABOUT 8 CELERY STALKS

CHICKEN WINGS
WITH BLUE CHEESE
DRESSING

I love the crazy combination of the hot spicy sauce (it's up to you how hot you make it), followed by a bite of creamy blue cheese that you've scooped up with a celery stick.

To make the dipping sauce, mash the blue cheese with a fork and mix with the yoghurt, lemon juice, garlic and olive oil. Season with salt and pepper and whisk lightly with the fork, leaving some chunky bits.

To make the coating sauce, melt the butter in a small saucepan until sizzling, then add the vinegar, Tabasco, sweet paprika and a little salt and let it bubble up for a minute or so.

Halve the chicken wings, so you have one tiny drumstick and another tiny wing. Pat the wings in the flour and season with salt and pepper. Fry in hot oil until they are deep golden, crispy and completely cooked through. Transfer them to a plate lined with kitchen paper to absorb the excess oil.

Toss the chicken in the butter coating sauce and serve immediately. Serve the blue cheese sauce and celery on the side for dipping.

Serves 2

2 SOFT RUMP STEAKS, *about* 120 g (4^1/2 oz) *each*
125 ml (^{1}/2 cup) RED WINE
2 LARGE GARLIC CLOVES, *lightly crushed with the flat*
of a knife
SPRIG OF ROSEMARY
3 TABLESPOONS OLIVE OIL
20 g (3/4 oz) BUTTER
2 FLOURY BREAD ROLLS, *halved*
CHOPPED CHILLIES IN OIL, *to serve* (PAGE 160)
LEMON WEDGES, *to serve*

PREGO ROLLS

This is probably a South African–Portuguese combination. Whatever their origins, I love prego rolls and actually crave them at times. The steaks should just be a couple of millimetres thick and the wine not be too heavy. The best bread rolls to use are the floury rosette type. You have to have everything ready, as the meat will only take a couple of minutes to cook and these really need to be eaten warm.

Marinate the meat in the wine, whole garlic cloves and rosemary for a couple of hours. Leave it covered in a cool place. If it is in the fridge, bring it back to room temperature before cooking.

Keep the marinade and pat the meat dry with kitchen paper. Heat a large non-stick frying pan to very hot and add 1 tablespoon of the olive oil. Fry the steaks quickly on both sides until cooked and lightly golden, sprinkling a little salt on the cooked side. Take care not to overcook and dry out the meat. Transfer the meat to a plate. Remove the rosemary sprig and quickly add the marinade to the pan with the butter. Return to the heat and cook until it bubbles up and thickens slightly.

Spoon some juice over the bottom half of each roll, top with a steak, drizzle over a little more juice and then dip the cut side of the roll top in the pan juice. Drizzle any remaining juice and about a tablespoon of olive oil over each steak. People can dress their rolls themselves with a bit of chopped chilli in oil, salt and lemon juice.

Serves 4

1 x 1.25 kg (2 lb 12 oz) CHICKEN WITH SKIN, *cut into 8 pieces*
3 SAGE LEAVES
1 CARROT, *cut into 2 or 3 chunks*
1 CELERY STALK, *cut into 3 or 4 chunks*
2 GARLIC CLOVES
2 EGGS
1/2 TEASPOON SWEET PAPRIKA
90 g (3/4 cup) PLAIN (ALL-PURPOSE) FLOUR
LIGHT OLIVE OIL *or* VEGETABLE OIL, *for shallow-frying*

FRIED CHICKEN

This is another great chicken recipe that makes two dishes in one go: fried chicken and a chicken soup. Use the broth to cook some pasta or rice and make a soupy meal. You can also add an extra egg to the leftover marinade and make a quick omelette for after your soup.

Rinse the chicken and put in a large saucepan with the sage, carrot, celery and one garlic clove. Cover with 1 litre (4 cups) of cold water and season with salt. Bring to the boil, uncovered, then lower the heat slightly to medium. Simmer for another 15 minutes, then remove from the heat. The chicken will be just boiled, not overcooked.

Remove the chicken with a slotted spoon to a plate and pat dry with kitchen paper. (At this stage you're left with the basis of a very good chicken broth in the saucepan. Add another cupful of water and simmer the soup for another 45 minutes. Store in the fridge or freezer until needed.)

Whip the eggs in a shallow bowl. Finely chop the remaining garlic and add to the egg with the paprika and a little salt. Put the chicken pieces in the egg, turning to coat them well, then leave to marinate for 10–15 minutes.

Put the flour on a flat plate. Heat enough oil for shallow-frying in a frying pan or wide saucepan. Lift the chicken out of the marinade, shaking off any excess egg, then pat in the flour, pressing down gently with your palm so that the flour sticks. Fry the chicken in the hot oil until it is deeply golden and crispy on both sides. Serve with lemon wedges if you like.

Serves 4

85 g (3 oz) BUTTER
1 ONION, *minced in a processor or very finely chopped*
250 ml (1 cup) TOMATO KETCHUP
2 TABLESPOONS WORCESTERSHIRE SAUCE
2 TABLESPOONS APPLE CIDER VINEGAR
4 TABLESPOONS BROWN SUGAR
80 ml (^{1}/3 cup) LEMON JUICE
80 ml (^{1}/3 cup) RUNNY HONEY
1 kg (2 lb 4 oz) BABY-BACK PORK RIBS,
  halved horizontally if large

BARBECUED
SPARE RIBS

These are those wonderful sweet ribs that you find at the steak houses in South Africa. They bring you just a great big rack of spare ribs and perhaps some garlic bread and you eat with your fingers. I love making this type of thing from time to time. These need a bit of marinating beforehand.

Heat the butter in a wide non-stick saucepan and sauté the onion over gentle heat until softened but not browned. Add the rest of the ingredients (except the ribs) and 250 ml (1 cup) of water to the pan and simmer for about 10 minutes until the sauce has thickened.

Put the ribs and the sauce in a large ovenproof dish so that they fit quite compactly and leave them in the fridge for at least a few hours.

The ribs are best cooked over a barbecue. Either heat a gas barbecue to medium-high or heat your coals. If using coals, let them begin to die down, making sure there are no flames as you don't want to burn the meat. Scrape off any excess marinade and barbecue the ribs until they are deep golden on both sides and charred in some places. Check that the pork is cooked all the way through to the bone. If there are any really thick ribs, cut them up individually and put them back over the coals.

Remove the ribs from the grill and put them back into the marinade in the dish. Add 125 ml (^{1}/2 cup) of water to the marinade. Put the dish on the barbecue and cook until the sauce boils and becomes sticky, thick and dark (the sauce must come to the boil and boil for a few minutes). Turn the ribs over a few times while you are reducing the sauce. Serve immediately, either cut up individually or in their racks.

Serves 10

1.25 kg (2 lb 12 oz) PIECE OF BEEF FILLET
1 kg (2 lb 4 oz) RIPE TOMATOES, *sliced*
A FEW SPRIGS OF ROSEMARY & SAGE
A FEW BAY LEAVES
4 RED ONIONS, *thinly sliced*
300 g (10^{1}/2 oz) UNSMOKED PANCETTA, *thinly sliced*
1 kg (2 lb 4 oz) SMALL SWEET POTATOES
2 GARLIC CLOVES, *chopped*
1^{1}/2 TEASPOONS DRIED OREGANO
JUICE OF 1^{1}/2 LEMONS
4 TABLESPOONS OLIVE OIL
10 LARGE FLAT FIELD MUSHROOMS

BARBECUED BEEF FILLET WITH SWEET POTATOES & GRILLED MUSHROOMS

My friend Jason made this years ago on a farm in South Africa. It was beautiful. The beef fillet is simply seasoned and spiced and then mummified in bacon before being seasoned and spiced again. It is then covered in sliced tomatoes and onions, wrapped in foil and placed under the red-hot wood coal. This is best served with baked sweet potatoes, next to the fire, under a star-filled African sky.

This is best cooked over a coal or wood barbecue. When it is very hot, put a rack over the barbecue and sear the fillet all over so it is golden. Remove from the heat. Lay down six pieces of foil, overlapping well, to make a rectangle at least 60 cm (24 inches) long. Arrange half the tomato slices in the middle and season with salt and pepper. Top with a sprig of rosemary, sage and a couple of bay leaves. Arrange half the onions over the top and season with salt and pepper. Arrange half the pancetta on top, slightly overlapping each slice, to make a rectangle.

Lay the fillet on top of the pancetta, sprinkling with salt and pepper. Wrap up the fillet in the pancetta from the bottom up and then lay the rest of the pancetta over the top. Repeat the onions and other ingredients in reverse order. Wrap up tightly in the foil (it's great if you have someone to help) and then roll a few more layers of foil around the meat, so you have a neat package. Cook directly in the barbecue coals for about 1^{1}/4 hours for rare beef and longer if you prefer. Turn the meat every 15 minutes or so during the cooking time.

Meanwhile, scrub the potatoes and prick the skins in a couple of places. Sprinkle with salt and wrap in foil. Bake among the coals for about 50 minutes, turning occasionally.

Combine the garlic, oregano, lemon juice and oil and season with salt and pepper. Brush over the mushrooms and grill on a rack over the hot coals for about 5 minutes on each side, or until they are cooked through, brushing with more marinade during cooking. Serve immediately.

Serves 8

2 kg (4 lb 8 oz) OXTAIL, *cut into 2.5 cm* (1 inch) *pieces*
125 g (1 cup) PLAIN (ALL-PURPOSE) FLOUR
6 TABLESPOONS OLIVE OIL
30 g (1 oz) BUTTER
3 CARROTS, *chopped*
2 CELERY STALKS, *chopped*
2 ONIONS, *chopped*
250 ml (1 cup) RED WINE
2 SPRIGS OF SAGE
2 BAY LEAVES
3 PARSLEY STALKS

OXTAIL

Ask your butcher to cut up the oxtail for you unless you have a professional cleaver at home (in which case, cut through the natural ridges of the oxtail to make pieces of about 2.5 cm/1 inch). This is lovely served with the sweet potatoes in orange juice (see overleaf) or just plain mashed potatoes. You could also use osso buco instead of the oxtail.

Bring a large saucepan of water to the boil. Add the oxtail and boil for about 15 minutes, skimming away the scum with a slotted spoon. Drain and rinse the oxtail, then pat dry. Put the flour on a flat plate and lightly coat the oxtail on all sides.

Heat half the oil in a non-stick frying pan and fry the oxtail until golden on all sides. Sprinkle with a little salt and pepper as you turn the pieces over. Fry in batches if necessary, adding extra oil if needed, to ensure the flour doesn't burn. Put the cooked oxtail in a casserole dish. Preheat the oven to 170°C (325°F/Gas 3).

Wipe out the frying pan with kitchen paper and heat the remaining oil and the butter. Add all the vegetables and a little salt and pepper and sauté for about 10 minutes, until softened. Add the wine and cook uncovered for a little longer until it has almost all evaporated. Add the vegetables and any cooking juices to the dish and add the sage, bay leaves, parsley, about 1.25 litres (5 cups) of hot water and a little more salt and pepper. Cover and put in the oven.

After 1 hour, add up to a litre or so of hot water (depending on how much has been absorbed) and continue cooking for another 2½ hours. Add another couple of cupfuls of water and cook for a final 30–40 minutes. It's important not to add all the water at the beginning or you'll end up with a soup.

You should have a meltingly soft dish: the meat should come away from the bone very easily, and there should be some thickened sauce with the vegetables to serve with the meat.

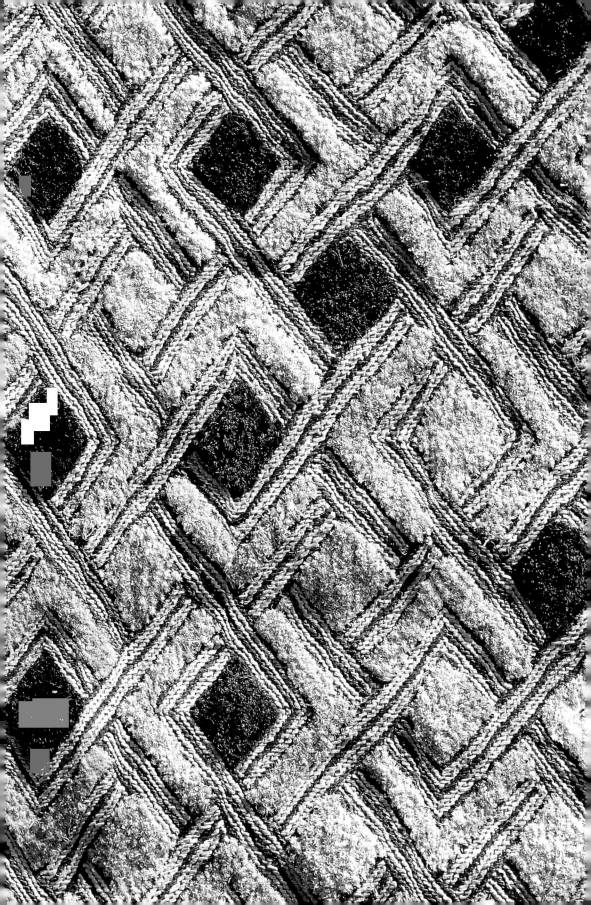

Serves 8

pastry
100 g (3¹/2 oz) COLD BUTTER, *cut into cubes*
100 g (3¹/2 oz) CASTER (SUPERFINE) SUGAR
230 g (8 oz) CAKE FLOUR *or* PLAIN (ALL-PURPOSE) FLOUR
¹/2 TEASPOON BAKING POWDER
1 EGG, *lightly beaten*

filling
750 ml (3 cups) MILK
75 g (2¹/2 oz) BUTTER
3 EGGS, *separated*
100 g (3¹/2 oz) CASTER (SUPERFINE) SUGAR
1 TEASPOON VANILLA EXTRACT
30 g (¹/4 cup) CORNFLOUR (CORNSTARCH)

1 TABLESPOON SUGAR
1 TEASPOON GROUND CINNAMON

MILK TART

Milk tart was something we ate often in South Africa; it was on the menu in many tea rooms and bakeries. You might like to make double the pastry and freeze it ready rolled-out in the tin so that you can whip it straight into the oven whenever you need to produce a pudding in a rush.

To make the pastry, mix the butter and sugar together with a wooden spoon until softened. Add the flour, baking powder and a pinch of salt and mix with your fingers until damp and sandy. Add the egg and knead very gently so that the pastry comes together. Flatten a little and wrap in plastic. Refrigerate for 1 hour before rolling out. Preheat your oven to 180°C (350°F/Gas 4).

Roll out the pastry on a floured work surface to line a 26 cm (10¹/2 inch) tart tin with sides at least 3 cm (1¹/4 inches) high. Line with baking paper, fill with baking beans or weights and blind bake for 20 minutes. Remove the beans and paper when the visible pastry is golden. Prick the pastry base a few times with a fork and bake for a further 10 minutes to dry out the bottom.

Meanwhile, make the filling. Put the milk and butter in a pan over medium heat to melt the butter. Whisk the egg yolks with the sugar and vanilla, then whisk in the cornflour. Add a ladleful of the hot milk to the eggs, whisking to avoid scrambling them. Add the rest of the milk, mix it all together well and leave to cool. Whisk the egg whites to soft peaks, then gradually fold into the filling. Pour into the tart case, sprinkle the sugar and cinnamon over the top and return to the oven for 30 minutes, or until it is set and just a bit wobbly. Cool before serving.

often
...
to the rocks
... they
...
didn't
rooms.

...aying
...DING
to the magnificence
...land.

19. Pan + Rucola (dream)
... Stinco di Vitello (?)
... Choc. Cake (Choc)

N.B
- choc sauce
- sweet potatoes
sweet rib
T.P
- Sautee Potatoes
- Luci's Chicken
- Fillet + feta
- Charlotte - double lunch
- Pumpkin + feta
- Green Salad f...

FOR KATY

FOR Lisa

After or before
that photo of Charlotte
with a ...
photo of Dad when...
photo of Pappa...
photo of Ise...

Serves 8

spice mix
5 CLOVES
1 CINNAMON STICK
6 ALLSPICE (PIMENTO) BERRIES *or* ¹/₂ TEASPOON
  GROUND ALLSPICE
RIND OF HALF A LEMON

syrup
JUICE OF 1 ORANGE
60 g (2¹/₄ oz) BUTTER
70 g (2¹/₂ oz) BROWN SUGAR
1 PINEAPPLE (about 1.2 kg/2 lb 12 oz)

cake
250 g (9 oz) BUTTER, *softened*
200 g (7 oz) BROWN SUGAR
3 EGGS
250 g (2 cups) CAKE FLOUR *or* PLAIN (ALL-PURPOSE)
  FLOUR
2 TEASPOONS BAKING POWDER
185 ml (3/4 cup) MILK

PINEAPPLE, CINNAMON & ALLSPICE CAKE

You can use any fruit you like here... raspberries, bananas, apples, pears or mangoes. I think apricots would be beautiful.

Preheat your oven to 200°C (400°F/Gas 6). To make the spice mix, put all the ingredients in a spice or coffee grinder and grind to a coarse dust.

Now make the syrup. Put the orange juice, butter and sugar in a small pan with ¹/₂ teaspoon of the spice mix and bring to the boil. Lower the heat and simmer for 8–10 minutes until you have a thick caramel syrup.

Line a 24 cm (9¹/₂ inch) springform tin with aluminium foil, so that the bottom and side are covered. Flatten the foil completely against the side so that it won't interfere with your cake. Peel the pineapple and cut into 1 cm (¹/₂ inch) slices. Cut each ring in half, either side of the core. Fit the pineapple pieces in the bottom of the tin in a single layer.

To make the cake batter, whisk the butter with electric beaters until fluffy and then beat in the sugar. Beat the eggs in one by one and then sift in the flour and baking powder. Mix to combine. Add the milk to thin out the mixture, beating it in well. Add 1½ teaspoons of the ground spice mix and give it a final whisk.

Pour the syrup over the pineapple in the tin, making sure that it covers it fairly evenly, and then spoon the cake batter over the syrup and smooth the top. Bake for about 1 hour 20 minutes, reducing the temperature to 180°C (350°F/Gas 4) after 10 minutes and covering the cake with foil after an hour. The cake should be deep golden on the top and a skewer inserted into the centre should come out clean. Remove from the oven and leave to cool slightly before turning out onto a serving plate. Remove the bottom of the tin and peel away the foil.

Serve with crème fraiche ice cream (page 379), or slightly sweetened whipped cream, or even completely on its own, very slightly warm.

Our garden in South Africa had a beautiful pomegranate tree. We loved picking the gorgeous heavy pomegranates and throwing them onto the white wall just behind the tree. Then we'd charge towards the ruby-streaked wall to gather our broken-up fruit, our bleeding jewels, that lay like coins sprayed from an open purse on our sun-warmed driveway, and suck out all the juice.

_ South Africa _

Serves about 10

4 EGGS, *lightly beaten*
250 g (2 cups) CASTER (SUPERFINE) SUGAR
185 ml (3/4 cup) SUNFLOWER *or* LIGHT OLIVE OIL
300 g (2^1/2 cups) CAKE FLOUR *or* PLAIN (ALL-PURPOSE)
  FLOUR
3/4 TEASPOON SALT
2 TEASPOONS BAKING POWDER
1 TEASPOON BICARBONATE OF SODA
2 TEASPOONS GROUND CINNAMON
400 g (14 oz) CARROTS, *peeled and grated*
55 g (^{1}/2 cup) CHOPPED WALNUTS

icing
180 g (6 oz) BUTTER, *softened*
250 g (2 cups) ICING (CONFECTIONERS') SUGAR
180 g (6 oz) CREAM CHEESE
3 DROPS VANILLA EXTRACT

CARROT
CAKE

This is one of those classic cakes that can disappear for a year or two, but I would always welcome back a slice from time to time with an afternoon coffee, or even for breakfast. This recipe is my friend Anette's. Every time she makes it people ask her for the recipe... so I did too.

Preheat your oven to 180°C (350°F/Gas 4). Grease and flour a 24 cm (9^1/2 inch) bundt pan or springform cake tin.

Whip together the eggs and sugar until creamy, then whisk in the oil. Sift together the flour, salt, baking powder, bicarbonate of soda and cinnamon. Add to the egg mixture and whisk to combine. Add the carrots and walnuts and mix through quickly with an electric mixer to make sure it is all properly combined. Scrape out the batter into the tin. Bake for about an hour, or until a skewer inserted into the centre comes out clean. The cake should have risen up impressively high. Cool a little before turning out onto a plate.

While the cake is baking, make the icing. Whip together the butter and icing sugar, mashing it together at first with a wooden spoon and then whisking until it is stiff. Quickly beat in the cream cheese and vanilla to just combine.

When the cake is cool, spread the icing over the top and side with a spatula (you don't need to spread it too smoothly, it looks better in peaks).

South Africa

Serves 4

500 ml (2 cups) POURING (SINGLE) CREAM
GRATED RIND AND JUICE OF 1 LEMON
1 TEASPOON FINELY CHOPPED SAGE LEAVES
160 g (²/3 cup) CASTER (SUPERFINE) SUGAR

LEMON
ICE CREAM

This is fresh and summery, eaten on its own or with a few berries and a biscuit. Or serve it on a platter with other lemony desserts for as many people as you like. Here I have added a couple of sage leaves to the ice cream. You could even try infusing the cream with some thyme, rosemary or other herbs, but you'll need to strain them out before churning.

Put the cream, lemon rind and sage in a saucepan and bring slowly to the boil. Set aside to cool and infuse the lemon and sage flavours into the cream.

Meanwhile, whisk the sugar with the lemon juice and 1 tablespoon of the cream mixture until the sugar dissolves. Add the remaining cream mixture and whisk well for a couple of minutes. Transfer to a bowl, cover and put in the freezer.

After an hour, remove the bowl from the freezer, give an energetic whisk with a hand whisk or electric mixer and return the bowl to the freezer. Whisk again after another couple of hours. When it is nearly firm, give one last whisk, transfer to a suitable freezing container with a lid and let it set in the freezer until it is firm.

Alternatively, pour the mixture into your ice-cream machine and freeze, following the manufacturer's instructions.

Makes 6

100 g (3¹/2 oz) BUTTER, *slightly softened*
100 g (3¹/2 oz) CASTER (SUPERFINE) SUGAR
1 LARGE EGG, *separated*
1 TEASPOON VANILLA EXTRACT
100 g (3¹/2 oz) CAKE FLOUR *or* PLAIN (ALL-PURPOSE)
    FLOUR, *sifted*
2 TEASPOONS FINELY GRATED LEMON RIND
1 TEASPOON BAKING POWDER
60 ml (¹/4 cup) MILK
JUICE OF HALF A LEMON

icing
1¹/2 TABLESPOONS LEMON JUICE
50 g (13/4 oz) ICING (CONFECTIONERS') SUGAR

LITTLE LEMON CAKES

These are light, fluffy and wonderful as part of a lemon platter. Instead of making the icing, you could halve and spread them with your favourite jam and a dollop of crème fraiche or whipped cream. If you don't have ramekins, you could make one large cake instead (use a 20 cm/8 inch tin).

Preheat your oven to 180°C (350°F/Gas 4). Butter and flour four 185 ml (3/4 cup) ramekins or moulds.

Cream the butter and sugar for a few minutes, then add the egg yolk and vanilla and whisk in well. Add the sifted flour, lemon rind and baking powder and fold in with a large metal spoon to incorporate it all. Pour in the milk and lemon juice and stir well. With clean beaters, whisk the egg white in a small bowl until it is very white and fluffy, and then fold it into the cake mixture with a metal spoon.

Drop 2 heaped tablespoons of mixture into each ramekin, ensuring that the base is covered and the mixture is even. Bake for about 30 minutes, until the cakes are deep golden and a bit crusty on the top, but still soft to touch and a skewer inserted comes out clean. Put the ramekins on a wire rack to cool completely. Remove the cakes by putting a spoon or knife down the side of each ramekin and lifting them out.

To make the icing, whisk the lemon juice and icing sugar together until smooth and fairly thick, adding a little more of either if it seems necessary. Put the cooled cakes on a flat plate, make a few holes with a skewer in the top of each one and dribble the icing over the top.

Makes 12

pastry
70 g (2¹/₂ oz) BUTTER, *slightly softened*
30 g (1 oz) SUGAR
70 g (2¹/₂ oz) PLAIN (ALL-PURPOSE) FLOUR
25 g (1 oz) GROUND ALMONDS

lemon curd
75 g (2¹/₂ oz) BUTTER
3 EGGS, *lightly beaten*
230 g (1 cup) SUGAR
JUICE AND FINELY GRATED RIND OF 2 LEMONS

LEMON
CURD TARTLETS

I love these tiny tartlets for a tea party or as part of a lemon dessert platter. If you have any leftover curd (you can always make double the quantity so that you have some to keep) store it in the fridge for up to a week and spread it on toast.

To make the pastry, cream together the butter and sugar with a wooden spoon. Add the flour, ground almonds and a pinch of salt and mix well, using your hands when it becomes a little stiff, until the pastry comes together. Flatten slightly, cover with plastic wrap and refrigerate for at least half an hour before using. (You can also freeze the pastry at this stage.)

Now make the curd. Melt the butter in a metal bowl over a saucepan of barely simmering water. Whisk in the eggs. Add the sugar and whisk until thoroughly combined. Whisking continuously, gradually add the lemon juice and zest. Cook over the simmering water for about 20 minutes, stirring often, until thickened. Cool to room temperature.

Preheat your oven to 180°C (350°F/Gas 4). Roll out the pastry thinly on a lightly floured work surface and cut out circles of pastry to line about 12 shallow tartlet tins. Line with baking paper, fill with baking beans or weights and blind bake for 8–10 minutes, or until the visible pastry is golden and cooked. Remove the paper and beans and cook for another couple of minutes to dry the bases. Remove from the oven and leave to cool before gently removing from the tartlet tins. When completely cooled, fill with lemon curd.

Makes about 1.3 litres

6 THIN-SKINNED LEMONS, *rinsed well*
1.25 kg (2 lb 12 oz) CASTER (SUPERFINE) SUGAR
1 VANILLA BEAN, *halved lengthways*

LEMON
VANILLA JAM

You must use good lemons here — I like the thin-skinned, bright ones that don't have much white pith. This is delicious spread on toast, brioche or pancakes. I love it spooned into tiny sweet pastry cases (like the ones opposite) and served as part of a lemon platter. You could also serve a little dish of this and a dish of mascarpone cheese next to a simple sponge cake for afternoon tea. Use the jam immediately or seal it in jars where it should keep, unopened, for many months. It is best to use a lot of smaller jars because, once opened, the jam should be eaten fairly quickly.

Cut the ends off the lemons, then slice them thinly. Remove all pips and then quarter the slices. Put them in a large, tall, heavy-based saucepan and add 1.25 litres (5 cups) water. Bring to the boil, then lower the heat and simmer uncovered for 45 minutes–1 hour or until the lemons are soft (this may take longer if you don't have a heavy-based pan). Make sure you cook on low heat as the water tends to splash up a bit and threaten to boil over. Watch it carefully towards the end and stir often. Add the sugar and vanilla bean and simmer uncovered for another 45 minutes–1 hour (you can add more water if it seems necessary). To test if the jam is ready, spoon a little onto a plate and tilt it. It should slide down with resistance and not just run down. If necessary, cook for longer.

If you are storing this, pour the warm jam into your sterilised jars (use a wide-necked funnel if you have one). Close the lids and turn the jars upside down, then cover them with a tea towel. Leave to cool completely before turning them upright. A vacuum should have formed on the lid. Store in a cool place and keep in the fridge once opened.

mulberries & silkworms

We had a huge mulberry tree at the bottom of our garden and spent ages collecting fresh leaves for our silkworms who lived part-time in a shoe box and breathed through the thousands of holes we had stabbed in the lid with a freshly sharpened pencil. We loved witnessing their various stages — from the steady munching of the mulberry leaves to the miraculous opening of the cocoons that would breathe out new lives.

The mulberries themselves were such a beautiful surprise, with their curly outsides that would explode into sweets in our mouths. At night we would take longer than usual washing our purply-black stained feet, before we could flop into bed, exhausted.

South Africa

Serves 8

250 g (9 oz) DIGESTIVE BISCUITS, *coarsely crushed in a blender*
125 g (4¹/2 oz) UNSALTED BUTTER, *melted,* PLUS A LITTLE EXTRA
750 g (1 lb 10 oz) CREAM CHEESE
250 g (9 oz) CASTER (SUPERFINE) SUGAR
4 EGGS
1 TEASPOON VANILLA EXTRACT
2 TEASPOONS CORNFLOUR (CORNSTARCH)
400 g (14 oz) FRESH *or* FROZEN BERRIES
1 TEASPOON FINELY GRATED LEMON RIND

BERRY CHEESECAKE

If you are using frozen berries, leave them in a bowl to come to room temperature before you start (you probably won't need to add any water when you sauté them later). Raspberries on their own are beautiful here, but choose your favourite berries or use a mixture. Blueberries, blackberries and strawberries all work well. You can leave out the cornflour when you heat the berries, if you prefer, but they won't hold onto the cake so well. Or simply serve a slice of plain cheesecake with a spoonful of berries on the side.

Preheat your oven to 180°C (350°F/Gas 4). Grease a 24 cm (9¹/2 inch) springform tin. Mix together the crushed biscuits and melted butter. Press the biscuit mix into the tin so that it covers the base and comes about two-thirds the way up the side, kneading down with your palms to push it along evenly.

Whisk the cream cheese in a bowl with 200 g (7 oz) of the sugar. Beat in the eggs one by one and then the vanilla until you have a smooth thick cream. Pour over the base and smooth the top with a spatula. Bake for about 40–50 minutes, until it is lightly golden in parts and wobbles only a little when you shake the tin. Cool completely, then chill in the fridge for a few hours.

Meanwhile, mix the cornflour with a couple of tablespoons of cold water until it is smooth. Pour into a saucepan to heat up, then add the berries, grated lemon rind and the remaining sugar — the amount of sugar may depend on the sweetness of the berries. Cook for a couple of minutes, adding some water if it seems too thick, to just combine everything and then remove from the heat before the berries collapse. Set aside to cool completely.

Carefully remove the ring from the cheesecake and spoon the berries over the top. Cut into wedges to serve. If you are not serving it immediately, keep the cake in the fridge.

Makes about 50

250 g (9 oz) BUTTER, *cut into small pieces*, PLUS ABOUT
  25 g (1 oz) EXTRA
750 g (6 cups) CAKE FLOUR *or* PLAIN (ALL-PURPOSE)
  FLOUR
460 g (2 cups) CASTER (SUPERFINE) SUGAR
1 TEASPOON SALT
2 TEASPOONS BAKING POWDER
400 ml (14 fl oz) MILK
2 TABLESPOONS WHITE *or* RED WINE VINEGAR

SUE'S
RUSKS

These are what we had in South Africa for breakfast, often dipped in warm milk or coffee. I love having a jar of them in the house always. They are crisp and rustic and beautiful. Sue says her kids always liked to scatter the remaining crumbs over their breakfast cereal.

Preheat your oven to 190°C (375°F/Gas 5). Mix the butter into the flour with your hands or in a blender. Add the sugar, salt and baking powder and then mix in the milk and vinegar until you have a smooth soft dough. Grease a large baking tray with butter and flour.

Roughly divide the dough into three portions. Wet your hands with a little cold water and quickly roll long dough sausages, each about 30 cm (12 inches) long. Your tray needs to be big enough to accommodate them — mine is 34 cm (14 inches) by 25 cm (10 inches) and looks very big when I put the mix in. Arrange the dough rolls parallel on the tray with a few extra dots of butter between them.

Bake for 45 minutes–1 hour until the tops are golden and crusty. Remove from the oven and turn the heat down to 150°C (300°F/Gas 2). The dough rolls will have joined together but their outlines will still be visible. Cut down their lengths to separate them, then cut each roll into 3 cm (1¼ inch) pieces. Don't touch them for now, leave them in their tray to cool a bit and make them more manageable. Then lift them up and break them in half through their middles so that they look rustic and imperfect. If you find it easier, begin with a knife, chopping through a little and then breaking them apart with your hands.

Return them to the baking tray (lay them on their sides) and the oven for about 30 minutes on each side to dry out a bit. They should be not too toasted, but crumbly and firm. Let them cool completely before storing in a closed container or paper bag, where they will keep well for up to five days.

WASHING LINES + WISHING WELLS

WASHING LINES + WISHING WELLS

When I drive along the country roads of Italy
I watch the hills and they look like women,
voluptuous women, wearing skin-tight velvet and
corduroy dresses to show their beautiful curves. I love
the faithful lifestyle... the way the milk joins the
coffee in the cup, the same way the beautiful words
join for music that a whole nation sways proudly to.
It makes me feel safe, as if I could walk with my eyes
closed and grope only onto the ropes of consistency
to find my way. That civilised apperitivo hour, just at
the special time of day when the sun may be going
down, making that ageing ochra and stone wall
that's holding together the piazza seem even more
magnificent. Just at that time of day I like to sip
prosecco with all the others and bite into something
small, perhaps an artichoke crostino. It makes me
happy, as if a box of inspiration had landed in my lap
and I want to hold it forever.

Makes 2 small loaves

15 g (¹/₂ oz) FRESH YEAST
3 TABLESPOONS OLIVE OIL
1 TEASPOON SUGAR
400 g (14 oz) BREAD FLOUR
1¹/₂ TEASPOONS SALT
50 g (13/4 oz) OVEN-ROASTED TOMATOES (PAGE 288)

OLIVE OIL
BREAD

This is an ideal picnic bread. It is great filled as a large roll, cut into slices for crostini or bruschetta, or just broken off to eat as it is. It is quite wonderful plain or with some chopped sautéed mushrooms, roasted tomatoes, olives, nuts or herbs mixed through before its second rising.

Put the yeast in a large bowl with the olive oil, sugar and 1 cup (250 ml) tepid water and mix together. Leave for 10–15 minutes until it starts activating and looks frothy.

Add the flour and salt and mix with your hands until it comes together. Turn out onto a work surface and knead for about 10 minutes, or until it is firm, smooth and elastic.

Put the dough back in the bowl and cover with a tea towel and then with a heavier towel. Put the bowl in a draught-free warm place for 1¹/₂–2 hours until the dough has puffed right up.

Knock down the dough by punching out all the air to bring it back to its original size. Divide it in half. Now is the time to mix through any ingredients that you will be adding — in this case the roasted tomatoes. Work each half with your hands to form two small baguette-shaped loaves. Scatter a little flour onto a baking tray large enough to hold both loaves. You could also line it with baking paper or oil. Put the loaves on the tray, cover loosely with the tea towel and leave in a warm place for 20–30 minutes. Preheat the oven to 220°C (425°F/Gas 7).

Take off the tea towel and bake the loaves for 20 minutes or so, until they are nicely golden both top and bottom, and the bottom sounds hollow when you knock on it. Cool slightly before serving.

Makes 16

225 g (8 oz) PLAIN (ALL-PURPOSE) FLOUR
225 g (8 oz) CHILLED BUTTER, *diced*
4–5 TABLESPOONS ICED WATER
375 g (13 oz) ENGLISH SPINACH LEAVES
100 g (3¹/2 oz) MOZZARELLA *(drained weight)*
1 TABLESPOON 'CREMA DI FUNGHI PRATAIOLI AL
   PROFUMO DI TARTUFO' *(cream of mushrooms with truffle)*
1 TABLESPOON OLIVE OIL
1 TEASPOON TRUFFLE OIL
1 EGG, *beaten, for brushing*

SPINACH &
TRUFFLE PIES

This recipe is from my brother-in-law, Marco, who has a lovely restaurant, the Taverna di San Giuseppe, in Siena. I always have these when I go there. You should be able to find a mushroom 'crema' perfumed with truffle in an Italian delicatessen. The one I use is a purée of porcini and other wild mushrooms.

To make the pastry, sift the flour and a pinch of salt into a bowl. Add the butter and stir through to coat it with flour. Add enough of the iced water to make the dough come together. Gather into a ball and transfer to a floured work surface. Flour your hands and form the dough into a block. Roll this out to make a rectangle about 1 cm (¹/2 inch) thick with the short side closest to you. Fold up the bottom third of the rectangle and fold down the top third. Seal the edges lightly with a rolling pin. Turn the dough through 90 degrees and roll it out again into a rectangle that is about 5 mm (¹/4 inch) thick. Fold as before, turn the dough and roll out again. Do this once more, then put the dough in a plastic bag and leave in the fridge for 30 minutes.

Blanch the spinach in boiling salted water for about 5 minutes, or until it is soft, then drain well and squeeze out the excess water. Pass half the spinach through a mincer with the mozzarella so that it is very finely chopped. Chop up the remaining spinach by hand to keep some texture in the filling (or chop it all by hand if you don't have a mincer). Mix in the mushroom 'crema', olive oil and truffle oil and season with salt and pepper.

Preheat the oven to 200°C (400°F/Gas 6). Line a baking tray with baking paper. Roll out the pastry to make a square just larger than 40 cm (16 inches). Trim away the edges to make a neat square. Now cut lengthways and breadthways to make 16 squares of 10 cm (4 inches) each.

Dollop a tablespoon of the spinach mixture in the centre of each square, then fold over to form a triangle, pressing the edges down to seal. Arrange the pies on the baking tray and brush the tops with beaten egg. Bake for 10–15 minutes or until they are golden and the undersides are also firm and golden. Leave them to cool a little, just so you don't burn your mouth.

Serves 4 as a side salad

40 g (¹/4 cup) SHELLED WHOLE ALMONDS
20 SHELLED PISTACHIO NUTS
1 GREEN APPLE, *cored*
3 TABLESPOONS EXTRA VIRGIN OLIVE OIL
1 TABLESPOON BALSAMIC VINEGAR
80 g (2³/4 oz) SMALL ENGLISH SPINACH LEAVES
50 g (1³/4 oz) PARMESAN OR MATURE PECORINO
    CHEESE SHAVINGS
50 g (1³/4 oz) FINELY SLICED BRESAOLA, *left whole or
    cut into thin strips*

BABY SPINACH,
BRESAOLA, APPLE
& NUT SALAD

Naturally, the oil and vinegar here can be adjusted to suit your personal taste. This is a simple, healthy and nutritious salad that will serve four as a side dish and two as a light main course.

Put the nuts in a frying pan over medium heat and dry-fry until they are lightly golden. Sprinkle with salt and leave on one side. Cut the apple into about 10 or 12 slices. Whisk together the olive oil and balsamic vinegar and season with salt and pepper.

Place all the salad ingredients in a large bowl, splash with the dressing and add any extra salt and pepper. Mix through and serve immediately.

Serves 2

1 LARGE JUICY RED POMEGRANATE
80 g (2³/4 oz) ROCKET (ARUGULA), *rinsed,
  dried and stalks broken off*
2 TABLESPOONS OLIVE OIL
1 TABLESPOON BALSAMIC VINEGAR
40 g (1¹/2 oz) PARMESAN CHEESE, *shaved*

ROCKET, PARMESAN &
POMEGRANATE SALAD
WITH BALSAMIC

This salad has a definite Italian-Lebanese feeling about it. I first had it at my friend Niki's house and I've been making it ever since. You might like to add some crisp cucumber, or anything else you think would go well.

Cut the pomegranate in half. Remove and reserve the seeds from one half, taking care not to get any of the white pith. Squeeze the juice from the other half with a lemon juicer. Arrange the rocket on two plates.

Mix together the olive oil and balsamic vinegar in a small bowl and whisk in the pomegranate juice. Season with salt and pepper.

Scatter the pomegranate seeds and parmesan shavings over the rocket and drizzle a couple of tablespoons of dressing over each serving. Serve immediately.

Makes about 320 g (11¹/2 oz)

1.5 kg (3 lb 5 oz) RIPE TOMATOES
125 ml (¹/2 cup) OLIVE OIL
2 GARLIC CLOVES, *lightly crushed*

OVEN-ROASTED
TOMATOES

These are an essential ingredient in my house. I would like to have a constant supply, but I don't always get round to it. They are fabulous alone on bread; or with mozzarella and a little pesto; beautiful on pasta with their own oil; and can be added to any antipasto or meze platter. They are also good on hamburgers, and can even be added to a saucepan of pan-fried chicken escalopes at the last moment. They just wear a more elegant and tasty coat than the ordinary versatile tomato. Don't worry too much about following the quantities and the first time you make them might be a bit stressful, but after a couple of times you'll know exactly when to shift them around and when to take them out of the oven. To the oil, you can add a bay leaf, a rosemary branch, a couple of sprigs of thyme and a couple of cloves of garlic or whatever else you choose. Fresh basil, parsley and coriander (cilantro) might be best mixed through at the last moment. Here I have estimated very ripe, smallish tomatoes of about 70 g (2¹/2 oz) each, just to give you a guideline.

Preheat the oven to 200°C (400°F/Gas 6). Line a 35 cm (14 inch) baking tray with aluminium foil, then brush the foil with oil to prevent sticking.

Rinse the tomatoes, pat dry and cut in half from their tops down. Pack them very close together, seeded side up, on the foil. Scatter with salt and pepper and bake for 15 minutes or until you begin to notice them sizzling or colouring. Reduce the oven temperature to about 150°C (300°F/Gas 2) and bake for another 1¹/2 hours or so, until they are golden around their rims and a little shrivelled, but not completely dried out. They should not be soggy and collapsed, but firm and less dry than the sun-dried tomatoes that we buy.

Remove the tomatoes from the oven in batches if necessary, leaving the underdone ones to roast a little longer. If you won't be serving them immediately, leave them to cool completely, then transfer them to a container suitable for the fridge. Pour the oil over the top and add the garlic and any other seasonings you're going to use. They will keep for a few days in the fridge. Add more oil if you like and then, when your tomatoes are used up, you can drizzle just the flavoured oil over pasta, rice, salad, bread or baked potatoes.

Serves 6 as a starter

18 PERFECT ZUCCHINI (COURGETTE) FLOWERS
3 EGGS, *separated*
100 g (3¹/2 oz) PLAIN (ALL-PURPOSE) FLOUR
125 ml (¹/2 cup) COLD SPARKLING WATER
60 ml (¹/4 cup) WHITE WINE
9 NOT-TOO-BIG ANCHOVIES, *cut in half*
125 g (4¹/2 oz) MOZZARELLA, *cut into 18 cubes*
CORN, SUNFLOWER *or* LIGHT OLIVE OIL, *for frying*
18 SAGE LEAVES, *rinsed and dried*

FRIED MOZZARELLA- & ANCHOVY-FILLED ZUCCHINI FLOWERS WITH SAGE LEAVES

This is beautiful. I was always impressed by this dish. It is something I have learned in Italy and will always keep in my long-term favourites file. I also like the flowers just plain, but definitely eaten as soon as fried and sprinkled with lemon juice and a little salt.

Remove the inner stamens from the zucchini flowers by opening them up carefully and gently twisting the stamens away. Drop the flowers into cold water and swish them through carefully with your hands. Scoop them up and leave them to drain or pat dry with kitchen paper.

Whip the egg yolks in a good-sized bowl. Add the flour, sparkling water and wine. Season with salt and whisk until fairly smooth. In a clean bowl, whisk the egg whites into stiff peaks, then gently fold into the batter.

Fill each flower with an anchovy half and a piece of mozzarella. Loosely twist the end of the flower to stop the filling falling out. Pour about 3–4 cm (1¹/2 inches) oil into a large saucepan and heat up until it is hot enough for deep-frying. Dip the filled flowers into the batter and fry, in batches, on both sides until they are golden and crispy. Take care not to overcrowd the pan. Remove them with a slotted spoon and drain on kitchen paper to soak up the excess oil. For the last 30 seconds, dip the sage leaves into the batter and fry them quickly on both sides. Add them to the zucchini flowers and serve immediately with lemon wedges and a small scattering of salt.

Serves 4

JUICE OF HALF A LEMON
2 ARTICHOKES
1–1.25 litres (4–6 cups) HOT VEGETABLE BROTH
3 TABLESPOONS OLIVE OIL
30 g (1 oz) BUTTER, PLUS 1 TEASPOON
1 SMALL ONION, *finely chopped*
2 ITALIAN SAUSAGES (about 85 g/3 oz each),
   skin removed and meat crumbled
2 GARLIC CLOVES, *lightly crushed*
A COUPLE OF THYME *or* TARRAGON SPRIGS
250 g (9 oz) ARBORIO RICE
30 g (1 oz) GRATED PARMESAN CHEESE,
   plus extra to serve

RISOTTO WITH ARTICHOKES & ITALIAN SAUSAGE

It is simple to throw together a broth — just put some water on to boil with a carrot and onion, celery and peppercorns. Add a bit more water than the recipe calls for and boil it up for at least half an hour. A broth adds depth to a risotto; however, you can also use water.

Run a bowl of cold water and add the lemon juice. Trim the artichokes of their tough outer leaves. Chop off about a third of the top spear. Cut off the stem, leaving about 3 cm (about 1 inch). Trim away the dark outer stem. Cut the artichokes in half vertically and scrape out the chokes. Slice each one into 8 or 9 thin slices and put them in the lemon water.

Put the vegetable broth or water in a saucepan, cover and bring to a simmer. Keep at simmering point while you make the risotto.

Heat the olive oil with the teaspoon of butter in a wide heavy-based saucepan or a frying pan with high sides. Sauté the onion until golden and then add the crumbled sausage. Continue cooking until golden, stirring often so it doesn't stick. Add the garlic, drained artichokes and the sprigs of thyme or tarragon. Sauté until the artichokes are slightly softened and lightly golden.

Add the rice to the pan, stir well and season with salt and pepper. Add about 1 cup (250 ml) of the hot broth or water, lower the heat to a simmer and cook, stirring often, until almost all the liquid has evaporated. Add more liquid and continue cooking, stirring regularly and adding more liquid as it is absorbed, for about 20 minutes, or until the rice is tender. The risotto should still have some liquid and the rice grains should be firm yet soft and creamy. Stir in the butter and cheese and serve immediately with extra parmesan.

Serves 6

3 TABLESPOONS OLIVE OIL
2 SMALL FRENCH SHALLOTS, *finely chopped*
500 g (1 lb 2 oz) ARBORIO *or* CARNAROLI RICE
600 ml (21 fl oz) CHAMPAGNE
50 g (1¾ oz) PARMESAN CHEESE, *grated, plus extra, for serving*
80 g (2¾ oz) UNSMOKED SCARMOZA OR CACCIOTTA
   CHEESE, *grated*
40 g (1½ oz) BUTTER

CHAMPAGNE
RISOTTO

This is elegant, delicate and so simple, and I think would beautifully precede a main course grilled (broiled) fish. People may appreciate smaller portions here, so it could serve even more. You could add an extra ingredient — a couple of shelled prawns (shrimp) or some asparagus — but I actually like the almost startling honesty of just Champagne. I have also seen a whisked egg yolk incorporated into the risotto at the last moment. It is not necessary to use the best Champagne; you could also use prosecco. You will need just a couple of cupfuls for the risotto, so you can have a glass yourself while you are stirring and definitely serve it with a glass or two as well. Scarmoza and cacciotta are types of dry mozzarella cheese.

Heat the oil in a large heavy-based saucepan with high sides. Sauté the shallots gently for 5 minutes until they are softened and slightly golden. Add the rice and cook, stirring, for 30 seconds or so, until it is well coated with the oil. Add 300 ml (10½ fl oz) Champagne, stir and let the rice absorb it before you add one ladleful of hot water. When it has been absorbed, add another ladleful, stirring continuously to prevent the risotto sticking. Continue cooking the risotto in this way, making sure the water is absorbed before the next ladleful is added. After about 20 minutes you should have added about 1 litre (4 cups) of water. Add salt to taste.

When the rice has absorbed all the water, add the remaining Champagne. Stir well and then stir in the parmesan, scarmoza and butter. Taste for salt again and serve immediately, with freshly ground black pepper and extra grated parmesan.

Serves 6

ABOUT 1 kg (2 lb 4 oz) SMALL FRESH SARDINES
1 LARGE HANDFUL WILD FENNEL *or* BABY
  FENNEL FRONDS
3 SLICES WHITE BREAD, *crusts removed*
185 ml (3/4 cup) OLIVE OIL
500 g (1 lb 2 oz) LINGUINI
2 GARLIC CLOVES, *lightly crushed with the flat
  of a knife*
1 SPRING ONION (SCALLION), *white part only,
  finely sliced*

PASTA WITH SARDINES & WILD FENNEL

This is lovely and quite delicate in its simplicity. It will make six filling portions. Use small sardines, up to about 12 cm (5 inches) long and around 30 g (1 oz) each. If you like a stronger taste, you could also add a few mashed-up anchovies. You will need a large handful of beautiful soft wild fennel here.

Fillet each sardine by cutting off the head and making a slit along the underside with a small sharp knife. Remove the guts, then remove the central bone by pulling it away by the tail with one hand while holding the sardine with the other. You will be left with two attached fillets.

Remove any tough stalks from the fennel, leaving them in wisps or breaking them up if they are very long.

Crumble the bread into coarse crumbs. Heat 3 tablespoons of the olive oil in a non-stick frying pan and fry the crumbs until they are deep golden and crisp. Remove to a small bowl. Cook the pasta in a large pan of boiling salted water, following the packet instructions.

Heat the remaining olive oil in a large non-stick frying pan. Add the garlic, fennel and spring onion and sauté for a few seconds to flavour the oil, then add the sardines. Continue to cook for a few minutes on a high heat, flipping them around in the pan, but taking care not to break them up. Cook for a couple of minutes until the fish are just opaque. Remove from the heat until your pasta is ready.

Drain the pasta but keep a cup or so of the cooking water. Add the pasta to the frying pan if it fits, if not, transfer the pasta and sardines to a large bowl and carefully toss together, adding some of the pasta cooking water if necessary. Serve immediately with a small handful of bread-crumbs and a grinding of black pepper over each bowl.

Serves 3

12 RIPE CHERRY TOMATOES, *halved*
ABOUT 30 BABY SALTED CAPERS, *rinsed and squeezed dry*
125 ml (1/2 cup) EXTRA VIRGIN OLIVE OIL
2 GARLIC CLOVES, *lightly crushed with the flat of a knife*
ABOUT 8 BASIL LEAVES, *torn*
300 g (10 1/2 oz) SPAGHETTI

DANIELE'S
TOMATO PASTA

Fresh tomato pasta is always good and very quick to prepare. Of course, you will need beautiful tomatoes as they won't be disguised by any cooking. You might like to try this with a dash of chilli as well.

Put all the ingredients except the spaghetti in a bowl and season with salt and pepper. Leave for at least an hour if possible to let the flavours mingle. Cook the spaghetti in a large pan of boiling salted water, following the packet directions. Drain and add to the tomato sauce, tossing well to coat the pasta. Serve immediately, with or without grated parmesan.

Giovanni's very soul is Italian. He loves a deep plate of pasta; says it puts him right. He taught our girls how to slurp spaghetti before they could even chew.

Serves 6

1 kg (2 lb 4 oz) RIPE TOMATOES
4 TABLESPOONS OLIVE OIL
A FEW BASIL LEAVES
JUICE OF HALF A LEMON
2 GARLIC CLOVES, *lightly crushed*
500 g (1 lb 2 oz) SPAGHETTI

FRANCO'S
TOMATO PASTA

Here is another version of an uncooked tomato sauce, which you can try in summer when tomatoes are at their very best.

Peel the tomatoes and cut them lengthways into long thin slices. Put in a bowl with the olive oil, basil, lemon juice and garlic and season with salt and pepper. If the tomatoes are at all bitter you could sprinkle a teaspoon or so of sugar over them. Toss them around a bit, then cover and leave in the fridge for 3 or 4 hours.

Remove from the fridge to come back to room temperature and remove the garlic cloves. Cook the pasta in boiling salted water, following the packet instructions. Drain well, toss with the tomatoes, add any extra salt and pepper and serve immediately, perhaps with a little extra olive oil on top.

Serves 4

650 g (1 lb 7 oz) CALAMARI, *cleaned*
  (about 400 g/14 oz cleaned weight)
4 TABLESPOONS OLIVE OIL
1 TABLESPOON CHOPPED PARSLEY
1 SMALL DRIED RED CHILLI, *chopped*
3 GARLIC CLOVES, *crushed*
125 ml (1/2 cup) WHITE WINE
1 TOMATO, *peeled and chopped*
250 ml (1 cup) FISH BROTH OR WATER
200 g (7 oz) ENGLISH SPINACH, *chopped*
350 g (12 oz) SPAGHETTI

JULIETTA'S PASTA WITH SPINACH & CALAMARI

This is a Mediterranean combination that works well and you might even like to serve it with a drizzle of chilli oil. The calamari and spinach is also very good served with rice, or on toasted bread. You can use squid instead of the calamari.

Cut the calamari into small pieces of 2–3 cm (about an inch). Gently heat 3 tablespoons of the olive oil in a frying pan. Add the calamari, parsley, chilli and two of the garlic cloves. Season with salt. Sauté over medium heat for 10 minutes or so, until the calamari is lightly golden.

Add the wine and, when that has evaporated, add the tomato and cook until reduced. Gradually add the fish broth or water, adding more as it is absorbed. Lower the heat, cover the pan and simmer for about 1 hour, topping up with a little water or broth as the liquid is absorbed.

Meanwhile, heat the remaining tablespoon of olive oil and garlic in another pan. Add the spinach and sauté until wilted. Remove from the heat and set aside.

About 10 minutes before the calamari is ready, add the spinach to the sauce and simmer uncovered for the last 10 minutes so that the flavours blend well. Check the seasoning.

Meanwhile, cook the pasta in boiling salted water, following the packet instructions. Drain well but keep a cupful of the cooking water.

Mix the pasta with the calamari, adding a little of the cooking water if you think it needs more liquid. Serve immediately with an extra drizzle of olive oil.

You will need 3 round pizza trays that are about 28 cm (11 inches) in diameter.

Crumble the yeast into a large bowl. Add the honey, 375 ml (1½ cups) warm water and about 150 g (1¼ cups) of the flour. Mix well with an electric mixer. Cover the bowl with a cloth and leave in a warm place for about 30 minutes, or until the yeast begins to activate. Add the remaining flour and 1 tablespoon olive oil and mix in (with the dough hook of the mixer or by hand) until the dough comes together. It may be necessary to add a drop more water or flour, but the dough should be soft and sticky, not dry. Add the salt and mix through thoroughly. Cover the dough and leave for about 10 minutes.

Lightly brush the pizza trays with olive oil. Gently extend one-third of the dough into each of the trays. Don't worry if it doesn't pull to the edge easily (it will become easier if you leave it for a bit). Leave uncovered for about 15 minutes and then work the dough with your hands, flattening it to the edge of the baking tray. Cover and leave to rise in a warm place for about 1–1½ hours or until the dough is nice and puffy.

Preheat the oven to 220°C (425°F/Gas 7) or to its hottest temperature. Season the tomato with salt and spread thinly over the bases, leaving a very thin border around the edge. Divide the mozzarella between two of the pizza bases, reserving a little.

To make the ham, artichoke and mascarpone topping, scatter ham pieces over one of the mozzarella-based pizzas. Scatter with artichokes and then with a little more mozzarella to prevent the ham from drying out. Dot the mascarpone over the top. Drizzle very lightly with good olive oil (or the oil from your artichokes).

To make the pancetta and rosemary topping, drape half the pancetta over the other mozzarella-based pizza and scatter with a little more mozzarella. Scatter the rosemary leaves over the top and drizzle lightly with olive oil.

To make the pepper, rocket and avocado topping, scatter the pepper over the last pizza. The remaining toppings will be added once the base is cooked.

Bake the pizzas for 10–15 minutes (depending entirely on the heat of your oven), or until the top is golden in parts and the bottom is lightly golden and firm. The two mozzarella pizzas are now ready to serve.

To complete the pepper pizza, scoop out the avocado flesh and add the lemon juice. Season with salt and pepper. Dot the avocado over the pizza, scatter with the rocket, olives, a dash of Tabasco and a drizzle of olive oil (if you are using chilli oil, leave out the extra olive oil). Serve quickly, before the rocket looks tired.

Serves 6

1 kg (2 lb 4 oz) SALT COD, *soaked in cold water for 2 days*
3 TABLESPOONS OLIVE OIL, *plus extra for shallow-frying*
4 RED ONIONS, *halved and thinly sliced*
2 TABLESPOONS BUTTER
3 GARLIC CLOVES, *crushed*
250 ml (1 cup) WHITE WINE
2 x 400 g (14 oz) TINS CRUSHED TOMATOES
60 g (1/2 cup) PLAIN (ALL-PURPOSE) FLOUR

BACCALA
WITH RED ONIONS

This is one of my mother-in-law's favourite ways of cooking baccala. She is an amazing cook: the grandmother cook that I always look for. This is a strong dish, I think, and not one that draws indifference. The cooked onions alone would go beautifully in an omelette, added in at the last moment onto the just setting egg, and are also great on bread even without the baccala. If you can, soak the salt cod under a dripping tap so the water is constantly changing. If you can't manage that, soak it for two days, changing the water regularly. You can taste a small piece of the fish to see how salty it still is and take care when you add extra salt to the sauce. This dish also works really well with tuna (obviously without the soaking beforehand).

Drain the fish well and cut into pieces about 4 x 6 cm (1½ x 2½ inches). Pat dry with kitchen paper. Heat the olive oil in a large frying pan and sauté the onions over medium heat for about 5 minutes until they begin to soften. Lower the heat and continue cooking for about 15 minutes, stirring often, until they are soft and richly coloured, then add the butter.

Add the garlic and, when it has coloured a bit, add the wine, season and continue cooking until the wine has evaporated. Add the tomato and a little more salt and pepper and simmer for about 5 minutes, until the tomato has softened a bit. The sauce shouldn't be too dry or too runny but just loose. Add a few drops of water if it seems dry, or cook for a little longer if it seems too runny.

Meanwhile, heat the extra olive oil in a non-stick frying pan over medium heat. Put the flour on a plate and dust the pieces of fish. Fry the fish in batches for about 8 minutes, or until it is golden on both sides (let it form a bit of a crust before you turn it over as it can be a bit crumbly). Put the cooked pieces on a plate lined with kitchen paper to absorb the oil.

Arrange the fish, skin side down, on top of the tomato and onions in the frying pan and spoon a little of the sauce over it. Heat through for a few minutes, shaking the pan from side to side to distribute the sauce, rather than turning the fish over and breaking it up. Serve immediately with some bread and a side salad. Some people also like this dish at room temperature.

Serves 4

3 TABLESPOONS OLIVE OIL
1 GARLIC CLOVE, *lightly crushed with the flat of a knife*
400 g (14 oz) TIN TOMATOES, CHOPPED
2 TABLESPOONS CAPERS
60 g (1/4 cup) PITTED GREEN OLIVES, *chopped*
2 TABLESPOONS CHOPPED FLAT-LEAF (ITALIAN)
    PARSLEY
30 g (1/4 cup) PLAIN (ALL-PURPOSE) FLOUR
8 RED MULLET FILLETS (about 30 g/1 oz each),
    all bones removed but skin left on

TRIGLIE AL POMODORO (RED MULLET WITH TOMATOES)

This is also good served at room temperature as an antipasto. It doesn't need much else to accompany it as a main course; just bread or maybe some boiled potatoes and a salad. You can use capers in vinegar (just drain them first), or the salted ones, rinsed.

Put the olive oil and garlic in a large saucepan over medium heat. When you can smell the garlic, add the tomatoes and a little salt and cook for about 10 minutes until the tomatoes have melted, adding about 1/2 cup (125 ml) of hot water towards the end of this time. Stir in the capers, olives and parsley.

Meanwhile, sprinkle the flour onto a flat plate. Lightly pat the fish fillets in the flour, season with a little salt and add to the tomato. Cook for about 8 minutes, turning them over once, until they are cooked. Check the seasoning and serve with black pepper and some bread.

Serves 2

1 TABLESPOON OLIVE OIL
20 g (3/4 oz) BUTTER, *plus an extra knob*
2 VEAL CHOPS, about 1.5 cm (5/8 inch) thick
6 SAGE LEAVES, *rinsed and dried*
1 GARLIC CLOVE, *crushed*
JUICE OF 1 SMALL LEMON
60 g (2¹/₄ oz) MASCARPONE

PAN-FRIED VEAL CHOPS WITH LEMON, SAGE & MASCARPONE

One of my favourite chefs in the world, Angela Dwyer, taught me this recipe. I love lemon; I love veal, sage and mascarpone; so it is unlikely that I wouldn't love the finished dish. You have to work quickly here so that the butter in the pan doesn't burn and the chops get nicely browned — so have everything ready before you start.

Heat the oil and butter in a large frying pan. When it is sizzling, add the chops and cook over high heat, turning over when the underneath is golden. Now add the sage leaves and garlic and season the meat with salt and pepper. Add another knob of butter to the pan to prevent burning. Take out the sage leaves when they are crisp and move the garlic around (or take it out if it starts to look too dark). You might like to turn the meat onto its fat side with a pair of tongs so that the fat browns.

Add the lemon juice to the pan and swirl it around, then add the mascarpone. If the veal is cooked, transfer it to a serving plate while you finish the sauce. If you think the veal needs longer, then leave it in the pan. It should be golden brown on the outside and rosy pink, soft, but cooked through on the inside. Add about 3 tablespoons of water to the pan and scrape up all the bits that are stuck to the bottom. Cook for another couple of minutes, then pour the sauce over the veal and scatter with the crispy sage. Serve immediately with some bread for the sauce.

Serves 4–6

8 LARGE CABBAGE LEAVES (*savoy or Chinese*)
50–60 g (2 oz) CAUL FAT (AVAILABLE FROM GOOD
     BUTCHERS)
5 TABLESPOONS OLIVE OIL
1.25 kg (2 lb 12 oz) BONED LOIN OF VEAL (*keep the
     bone if possible*)
4 TABLESPOONS MILD MUSTARD (grainy or smooth)
8 THIN SLICES UNSMOKED PANCETTA *or* LARDO
     DI COLLONATA
500 ml (2 cups) WHITE WINE

VEAL LOIN WITH MUSTARD, PANCETTA & CABBAGE

This is a dish my sister-in-law Luisa taught me. It is a great dinner: it looks impressive but, once you've done the first bit of preparation and wrapped the meat up, you can just put it in the oven and not think about it too much. If you can find lardo di collonata then use that, otherwise pancetta is just fine.

Slice away the bottom third of the thick stem of the cabbage leaves so that they sit flat. Bring a saucepan of lightly salted water to the boil. Blanch the cabbage leaves for a couple of minutes to soften them (depending on their thickness). Drain and spread them out flat on a clean tea towel to cool.

Soak the caul fat in a bowl of warm water for 10 minutes or so. Drain, squeeze out the water and carefully lay it down flat on the work surface. Keep it in one piece if possible, if not, in overlapping pieces.

Pour the olive oil into a rectangular ovenproof dish that can also be put on the stove-top. Put the dish on the stove over fairly high heat. Add the veal and brown on all sides. Remove the dish from the heat and cool the veal slightly. Transfer to a wooden board and season all over with salt and pepper. Spread the top with half the mustard.

Preheat your oven to 200°C (400°F/Gas 6). On a space next to the veal or on another board, arrange about four of the cabbage leaves, overlapping them to form a bed. Lay half of the pancetta strips next to each other on top to form a smaller layer over the cabbage. Put the veal, mustard-side down, over the pancetta. Spread the top with mustard and then arrange the remaining pancetta over the veal loin, enclosing it like a neat wrapping. Put the remaining cabbage leaves over the top (or as many as you will need to enclose the veal), tucking them in neatly. Put the whole package onto the caul fat and wrap it up securely so that it is completely enclosed in whichever way you see best. The caul fat will hold, but you can tie a bit of string around the meat just so that you can turn it around easily in the oven dish.

Put the meat back into the oil in the oven dish and add any bones to the dish. Bake in the oven for about 1¹/₂ hours. Halfway through cooking, when the bones have browned a bit, turn the meat over and add the wine. Continue cooking until the outside is browned.

Remove the meat from the dish, remove the string and leave it for 10 minutes or so before slicing. Serve with the pan juices.

...so, I learnt to make the right bowl of pasta, the one Giovanni's very bones know, standing by his mamma's side. But I still love to go to her. With no effort or fuss at all, she runs the show in her soft and matriarchal manner, settling her four sons and chef husband into their places. Her real-life knowledge of the soups and sauces, her earth instinct and her lifetime behind her, have armed her. Her wooden spoon is her sword, defending and letting her rise, just like her olive oil bread, to every occasion.

Serves 4–6

LEAVES FROM 1 *or* 2 ROSEMARY SPRIGS, *finely chopped*
6 SAGE LEAVES, *chopped*
LEAVES FROM 1 *or* 2 THYME SPRIGS, *chopped*
3 GARLIC CLOVES, *chopped*
1 x 1.8 kg (4 lb) VEAL SHIN
4 TABLESPOONS OLIVE OIL
1 SMALL ONION, *cut into quarters*
1 CELERY STALK, *cut in half*
1 CARROT, *chopped*
500 ml (2 cups) WHITE WINE
30 g (1 oz) BUTTER

STINCO DI VITELLO
(SHIN OF VEAL)

You could also add some other herbs instead of, or with, these and also a little finely grated lemon rind in the herb mix. Serve with cannellini bean purée (see over).

Preheat the oven to 220°C (425°F/Gas 7). Combine the rosemary, sage, thyme and garlic in a bowl. Put the veal shin on a board and, with a sharp knife, make two small slits on the meaty side. Try to judge exactly where they would meet up on the other side of the veal and make a couple of slits there too. Poke the knife through a bit to open up a canal, then take the handle of a wooden spoon and push it all the way through. Repeat with the other slit, to make a second canal. Push the herb garlic mix into these canals with the handle of the wooden spoon (the mixture will flavour the inside of the meat without burning during the long cooking).

Put the veal in an oven dish and drizzle all over with the olive oil. Bake in the oven for about 20 minutes to brown on both sides. Remove and season the outside all over with salt and pepper. Add the vegetables and wine to the dish and return to the oven for about 15 minutes, or until it starts bubbling up. Cover the dish with aluminium foil, lower the oven temperature to 180°C (350°F/Gas 4) and cook for another 2½ hours, or until it is very soft, turning the meat over a couple of times and basting. Remove the foil and cook for a little longer on each side to brown a little more, making sure it doesn't dry out. Transfer the meat to a serving dish. Put the oven dish directly over heat on top of the stove. Add the butter to the dish and scrape up any tasty-looking bits that are stuck to the bottom. Let it bubble up and reduce a bit to make a slightly thickened sauce.

Carve the meat away from the bone, then slice up thickly into pieces or chunks. Serve with the vegetables and some pan juices drizzled over the top.

Serves 12

40 g (1¹/₂ oz) AMARETTI BISCUITS
6 JUICY BUT FIRM, RED PLUMS
ABOUT 40 g (1¹/₂ oz) BUTTER, DICED
ABOUT 30 g (1 oz) CASTER (SUPERFINE) SUGAR
3 TABLESPOONS VIN SANTO

mascarpone cream
200 ml (7 fl oz) WHIPPING CREAM
250 g (9 oz) MASCARPONE
2 TABLESPOONS ICING (CONFECTIONERS') SUGAR
1 TEASPOON VANILLA EXTRACT

BAKED AMARETTI
& VIN SANTO PLUMS WITH
MASCARPONE CREAM

I like to eat this when the plums are warm, and I sometimes have it with a slice of pandoro or panettone. If the season is right, you can use peaches or nectarines instead of the plums. Save any leftover amaretti crumbs to sprinkle over ice cream.

Preheat your oven to 200°C (400°F/Gas 6). Crush the amaretti biscuits to coarse crumbs. Cut through the plums all the way around through to the stone. Hold the plum in your palm and twist the other half away so that it comes off smoothly. Sit the plums cut side up in a baking dish. Remove the stones with a teaspoon, twisting the teaspoon a little deeper than the natural cavity to make it a bit bigger and letting any juice dribble into the baking dish.

Spoon a heap of amaretti crumbs over the plums, so they settle into the cavities and over the tops (keep any leftover). Dot a little butter over each plum top and scatter with sugar. Scatter the rest of the sugar and butter around the plums with the vin santo. Bake for 15 minutes or until the liquid starts to get a bit of a caramel look, then add about 80 ml (¹/₃ cup) hot water around the plums. Bake for another 15 minutes or so, until the tops are golden and crusty and the plums are soft but still in shape. Remove from the oven.

To make the mascarpone cream, whip the cream, mascarpone, sugar and vanilla together until smooth and beautifully thick. Serve a plum half with a good spoonful of mascarpone cream and any pan juices dribbled over the top.

FERIAE MATRICULARUM MM

TEATRO DEI RINNOVATI

Nelle sere del 15-16-17 Maggio
il Princeps e la Balìa
presentano

"LA TARGA VOGLIO!"

ovvero

"Cresce solo nel giardino del Rettore..."

Operetta Goliardica in due atti, tre verbali e una targa

ATTO
CO IMPERATORE
CONQUISTATORE
E CHE HA PIANTATO
HA PERPETRATO...
L'ONNIPOTENTE
SISTENTE
A' ANDARE
E...

CARDI...   SEMPRE PIENE...   OZZO   VITELLOZZO   BANCO LIBERO...   NON PASSANO MAI
ANDRASSI...   SE ERO FURBO...   PONE   TONTO...   BANC-ADATI...   FA LE FERIE UN ALTR

AR UN D...   MORINO   BANCO...   GLI ANNI NE
DI LAUREARSI NON SE LA SENTE...   BUBBA   BANC-H...   IL DIO DELLA FA
     BANC-ONE...   IL GOLIARDO
FATE TUTTI COCCODÈ...   BOCCALONE PRENCE   BANC-AROTTA...   SEMPRE STREGA
ALLE SCENE FACCIO UN FIGLIO...   EMILIO   BANC-ARIO...   PER DA
SÌ, ORA TROMBO, MA DOVE...   BRODO
ASCO SÒ DIVENTATO...   BIRILLO   AMÈ...   NEL
TRA DUE FETTE DI PANE...   SALAME   MIGAR...
SENZA SCUOLE CHE FAREI...   AGNUSDEI   BALCUL...
DELLA MENS SANA...   BRADIPO   ASPIDI...
DALLA SÙ CITTA PARECCHIO...   VECCHIO   EUNUCO...
     ECONOMO...
SO' MATTO E NEMME...   MITINO   VICE-ECONOM
LA BALÌ NO, GRAZI...   NOTTO   ADDETTI ALL
TTE SEMP...   DIRO
AL F...   LA PANCIA   CIUFA

E ESAMI E CE L
ME PIACE IL...

ONDE

UN TO... NELL

OLA

Serves 8–10

100 g (3½ oz) BUTTER, *slightly softened*
85 g (3 oz) CASTER (SUPERFINE) SUGAR
150 g (5½ oz) PLAIN (ALL-PURPOSE) FLOUR
30 g (1 oz) UNSWEETENED COCOA POWDER
1 EGG, *beaten*

filling
3 EGGS, *beaten*
140 g (5 oz) CASTER (SUPERFINE) SUGAR
1 HEAPED TEASPOON FINELY GRATED ORANGE
　RIND
750 g (1 lb 10 oz) SMOOTH RICOTTA CHEESE
1 TABLESPOON LEMON JUICE
2 TABLESPOONS ORANGE JUICE

RICOTTA TART
WITH A CHOCOLATE CRUST

This is a typical southern combination of flavours: ricotta, the burstingly ripe oranges and, every Italian's obsession, chocolate. It is quite simple to make, so don't be intimidated by the thought of the pastry crust. If it seems too soft, just add more flour as you're rolling it, then lift it over your rolling pin and gently lower it into the tin. If it breaks, just patchwork it in.

To make the pastry base, use a food processor to mix together the butter and sugar until pale and creamy. Sift in the flour and cocoa and then beat in the egg to make a nice soft pastry. Scrape out onto plastic wrap, flatten into a disc and wrap up. Refrigerate for about an hour.

Preheat your oven to 180°C (350°F/Gas 4). Roll out the pastry on a lightly floured work surface until large enough to line a 24 cm (9½ inch) loose-bottomed tart tin or springform tin with high sides. Line the pastry with baking paper and baking beans or uncooked rice and bake for about 20 minutes. Remove the paper and beans and bake for a further 5 minutes to slightly dry the base.

For the filling, whisk together the eggs and sugar until thick and creamy. Whisk in the orange rind and ricotta until smooth. Whisk in the lemon and orange juice and scrape into your pastry case. Bake for about 30–40 minutes, or until the top seems set and is lightly golden here and there. Cool before cutting into portions. This can be served slightly warm, at room temperature or even cold from the fridge.

Serves 12

500 ml (2 cups) WHIPPING CREAM
6 EGGS, *separated*
230 g (1 cup) CASTER (SUPERFINE) SUGAR
ABOUT 125 ml (1/2 cup) MARSALA
1 LONG ESPRESSO COFFEE (60 ml/1/4 cup)
30 g (1 oz) BITTERSWEET CHOCOLATE, *coarsely
grated or chopped*

ZABAGLIONE
SEMIFREDDO

You might like to serve this with a few biscuits on the side (you can even use a firm biscuit rather like a spoon, to scoop up the semifreddo). Don't be discouraged as you are whipping the eggs: they will become very thick and fluffy eventually. The bowl you whip the egg yolks in must sit comfortably over the pot of simmering water. You can make this in 12 individual pudding pots that are freezer suitable or one large loaf mould.

Whip the cream until it is very thick, ribbony and almost buttery looking. Put it in the fridge for now and wash your beaters. Put the egg whites in a large bowl and leave aside for now.

Put the egg yolks in a wide, heatproof bowl. Add the sugar, Marsala and coffee and whisk together well. Half fill a saucepan with water and bring to the boil, then lower the heat to very low and sit the bowl over the simmering water. The water must not touch the bottom of the bowl, so tip out a little bit if necessary. Start whisking and continue until the zabaglione is very thick and ribbony and looks almost like marshmallow. It should cling to your whisk as you work. (The egg on the side of the bowl may start to look like scrambling as it gets close to ready, so just keep whisking this back in well.) Remove from the heat and leave to cool for a bit, mixing now and then.

Whip the egg whites to very fluffy stiff peaks and gently fold the slightly cooled zabaglione into the egg whites. Then fold in the cream with a large metal spoon. Hold the bowl firmly with one hand and fold with the other in long sweeping circles to incorporate all the cream, egg whites and zabaglione smoothly, without deflating the texture.

With the large spoon, dollop the mixture into twelve 180 ml (6 fl oz) pudding pots or ramekins so that they are very full and peaking over the rims. Or spoon it into one large serving dish that is suitable for the freezer. Put straight into the freezer and freeze for a few hours before serving. Serve either directly from the pots, with a scattering of chocolate over the top, or spoon out with a large tablespoon in one swift scoop. Either way, the zabaglione should be taken out of the freezer 5–10 minutes before serving so that it is not rock hard.

SUITCASE OF RECIPES

_(307)_

Souvenirs and memories from my travels are all around me. I remember struggling back with an overweight iron tortilla machine, fabrics that I had bartered off certain beaches, and spices and wooden boxes that now hold my ingredients. And always there would be pages of recipes flapping everywhere, flavours and tastes hastily jotted down while sandwiched between rows of people and ingredients at markets. Beautiful spices that I might never use but had to have, and some songs that crocheted all these memories together.

My diaries held my memories when I wanted to record the atmosphere and my feelings — walking along sand and smelling vanilla tea and oranges; eyeing street vendors selling a slice of their souls; and longing to know every last drop of what that Mexican had folded in my meat, lime, mayonnaise, lettuce and chilli torta. Always squeezing out the last details from people; from those families that interested me, sitting around their tables for hours and just watching. I could excuse myself, blaming lack of language for irrelevant questions. I would come home, luggage fat to bursting on the conveyor belt, anxious to unwrap my memories. I found this recharges my soul, and longed to return to those moments when my bare feet played with the sand under the table and my tongue danced with chilli and ginger.

Serves 4

4 cm (1¹/₂ inch) PIECE OF GALANGAL *or* GINGER, *peeled and sliced*
SMALL BUNCH OF CORIANDER (CILANTRO)
4 MAKRUT (KAFFIR) LIME LEAVES, *torn*
1 STEM LEMON GRASS, *halved lengthways*
3 TABLESPOONS FISH SAUCE
JUICE OF 2 SMALL LIMES
400 ml (14 fl oz) COCONUT MILK
250 g (9 oz) SKINLESS CHICKEN BREAST, *cut into thin strips*
1 RED CHILLI, *seeded and sliced*

TOM KA GAI
(THAI CHICKEN SOUP WITH COCONUT MILK, LIME & CORIANDER)

I just wouldn't cope with not knowing how to make some version of this soup. I love it. You can add a few mushrooms, a couple of fresh spinach leaves or some slices of zucchini (courgettes) in with the chicken. Also wonderful instead of the chicken is to cook some large, shelled prawns (shrimp) on a barbecue or griddle pan and toss them into the soup just before serving. The fish sauce is the salt in this soup so adjust the quantities according to your taste (and the same with the chilli). I like it not too strong. Keep the coriander stems in your freezer to add flavour to a broth or stew.

Put the galangal, coriander roots, lime leaves, lemon grass and 1 litre (4 cups) water in a saucepan and bring to the boil. Add the fish sauce and lime juice, lower the heat and simmer for 10 minutes. Remove the coriander roots. Add the coconut milk, bring back to the boil and boil for a couple of minutes. Add the chicken pieces and cook for just a minute or so, until the chicken is soft and milky looking and cooked through. Throw in the chilli and mix through. Serve in bowls with the coriander leaves roughly chopped and scattered over the top.

Serves 4–6

600 g (1 lb 5 oz) SKINNED SALMON FILLET
JUICE OF 4 LIMES
2 *or* 3 RED CHILLIES, *seeded and finely chopped*
2 TABLESPOONS CHOPPED CORIANDER (CILANTRO)
1/4 TEASPOON GROUND CUMIN
2 GARLIC CLOVES, *very finely chopped*
4 cm (1 1/2 inch) PIECE OF GINGER, *peeled and grated*

SALMON CEVICHE WITH CORIANDER, CHILLI & LIME

This is a wonderful dish of my friend Ana's that, thank goodness, has managed to grace our table many times. If you love every single ingredient that goes into something, how can you not love the finished dish? Changing quantities here is very simple: just add more of anything you like. You could also add a little olive oil if you are not using an oily fish such as salmon. Ana says ceviche is often eaten in Peru, using all kinds of fish: you can try prawns (shrimp), squid, mussels, oysters and just about any other fish fillet. This could be served with some firm green leaves and sliced red onions as a salad or with boiled potatoes. It would serve six as an antipasto or four as a salad or light main meal. Ceviche should be prepared at least four hours before you want to eat, to allow the flavours to mingle well and for the fish to 'cook' in the lime juice. It is even good the next day.

Remove any bones from the salmon (you can check for bones by stroking the salmon up and down). Slice it into pieces about 1 cm (1/2 inch) thick and put in a wide, non-metallic bowl.

Pour the lime juice, chilli, coriander, cumin and garlic over the fish and season with salt and pepper. Take the grated ginger between your fingers and firmly squeeze the juice over the salmon (discard the pulp that's left). Mix through gently, cover with plastic wrap and refrigerate for at least 4 hours before serving.

Serves 4

4 RED PEPPERS (CAPSICUMS), *cut in half lengthways and seeds removed*
2 TABLESPOONS OLIVE OIL
2 GARLIC CLOVES, *lightly crushed with the flat of a knife*
1 SMALL RED ONION, *sliced*
4 RIPE TOMATOES, *peeled and chopped, or* 400 g (14 oz) TINNED TOMATOES, *chopped*
300 g (10^1/$_2$ oz) PLAIN GREEK YOGHURT
40 g (^{1}/$_3$ cup) PITTED BLACK OLIVES, *roughly chopped*
FINELY GRATED RIND OF 1 LEMON
LEAVES FROM 2 ROSEMARY SPRIGS, *finely chopped*

RED PEPPER SOUP
WITH OLIVES, LEMON RIND
& YOGHURT

You can add any flavours you like to the base of this soup. Here, I use fresh rosemary and serve the soup with a yoghurt, black olive and lemon flavour. You might like to use another herb like fresh basil with a swirl of cream, or try adding a good kick of chilli oil to serve. You could even add a drop of truffle oil and a couple of grilled prawns (broiled shrimp). Serve with or without the yoghurt.

Preheat the grill (broiler) to high. Line a large oven tray with foil and arrange the peppers, skin side up, in a single layer. Grill for about 30 minutes until the skin has darkened in places and swelled up and the peppers are soft. You might need to move them around on the tray so they are evenly grilled or remove the halves that are blackened and leave some in for longer.

Transfer the peppers to a bowl, cover with plastic wrap (or put in a plastic bag and seal) and leave to sweat for 10 minutes to make peeling easier. Peel off the skin.

Heat the olive oil in a large saucepan and sauté the garlic and onion for about 5 minutes. Add the tomato and cook until it begins to bubble. Add the pepper halves, tearing them into large chunks as you put them in the pan. Season with salt and pepper. Add 750 ml (3 cups) water and bring to the boil, then lower the heat, cover the pan and simmer gently for about 30 minutes. Remove from the heat and purée. The soup should be fairly thick: if it seems too watery, simmer uncovered for a while longer. If it seems too thick, add a little more water.

Check the seasoning and serve the soup hot with a dollop of yoghurt and a sprinkling of chopped olives, lemon rind and rosemary.

Serves 6

350 g (12 oz) COUSCOUS
200 g (7 oz) OVEN-ROASTED TOMATOES (page 288),
    halved or quartered if large, plus their oil
1 LEBANESE (SHORT) CUCUMBER, *unpeeled and diced*
4 SPRING ONIONS (SCALLIONS), *chopped*
25 g (¹/2 cup) CHOPPED MINT LEAVES
3 TABLESPOONS LEMON JUICE
80 ml (¹/3 cup) OLIVE OIL
120 g (4 oz) GOAT'S CHEESE (soft or a little harder), *crumbled*

COUSCOUS
SALAD

The original version of this salad also uses broken-up pieces of pitta bread: this is a Middle-Eastern variation. The oven-roasted tomatoes are wonderful here (make them a day or so in advance, so they flavour the oil nicely) and you can vary the ingredients with different cheeses or herbs from time to time. This works very well served with yoghurt-marinated lamb. The dressing is light and not overpowering, so if you are serving the salad on its own, you could add a little extra lemon juice and olive oil.

Put the couscous in a large bowl and season well with salt and pepper. Add a splash of the oil from your oven-roasted tomatoes and 500 ml (2 cups) of just-boiled water. Stir, cover and leave to cool completely, fluffing it up gently now and then, so that the bottom does not become a stiff pudding.

Add the cucumber, spring onions, mint and lemon juice to the couscous. Add the tomatoes and the rest of their oil, topping up with the extra olive oil if you don't have enough from the tomatoes, and stir through well. Add the goat's cheese and stir through carefully, especially if it is soft.

Serves 6

dressing
2 SOFT ROSEMARY SPRIGS, *rinsed*
2 GARLIC CLOVES
ABOUT 8 OIL-PACKED ANCHOVY FILLETS, *drained and chopped*
1 HEAPED TABLESPOON DIJON MUSTARD
2 TABLESPOONS LEMON JUICE
90 ml (3 fl oz) VEGETABLE OIL
90 ml (3 fl oz) OLIVE OIL
2 EGGS, *at room temperature*

salad
1 FENNEL BULB, *halved and very finely sliced*
ABOUT 100 g (3½ oz) RADICCHIO *or* TREVISE, *torn into large chunks*
ABOUT 250 g (9 oz) FIRM INNER LETTUCE LEAVES
2 CELERY STALKS, *finely sliced*

CODDLED
EGG & ANCHOVY
SALAD

This is how my friend Jo makes her salad. She is an exceptional cook, full of enthusiasm and fun. She says she also likes this dressing with warm asparagus, broad beans and peas. I find it also goes well with olives and fresh raw vegetables for dunking into the sauce, or just with a plain steak and some fat chips for dipping. This will make a couple of cups of dressing that you can use as you like.

Bring about 750 ml (3 cups) of salted water to the boil and dunk the rosemary and garlic in the water a few times to soften them slightly. Strip the rosemary leaves off the stem and chop very finely with the garlic. Put in a bowl.

Whisk in the anchovies, mustard and lemon juice, a few grindings of black pepper and a little of each of the oils. Whisk well until it all comes together, a bit like mayonnaise.

Meanwhile, lower the eggs into the boiling water and boil for 3 minutes. (To be perfect, all of the white and a fine layer of yolk should be set; the rest of the yolk should be soft.) Rinse under cold water until cool enough to peel. Add to the dressing, whisking to break the eggs into small bits. Add the rest of the oil, whisking continuously until completely combined. Whisk in a teaspoonful of warm water to finish the dressing.

Put all the salad ingredients in a large bowl. Splash the dressing over the top, tossing well so that all the leaves carry a heavy coat of dressing, and serve immediately.

Serves 6

2 RED ONIONS, *chopped*
2 TEASPOONS SALT
5 TABLESPOONS OLIVE OIL
2 LARGE GARLIC CLOVES (*1 chopped, the other left whole*)
1 LARGE RIPE TOMATO, *peeled and chopped*
500 g (2²/3 cups) BROWN LENTILS
750 g (3³/4 cups) LONG-GRAIN RICE
JUICE OF 1¹/2 LEMONS
1 SMALL RED CHILLI, *seeded and finely chopped*
150 g (5¹/2 oz) PLAIN GREEK YOGHURT

LENTILS,
RICE & RED ONION
SALAD

This is more or less what they make in Peru: I have just added the yoghurt. The red onion salad gives the lentils such a lift and is also very good served with grilled (broiled) foods. I love this after it has been marinating for a few hours, even overnight, and has taken on a special fuchsia tone.

Rinse the onions and drain in a fine sieve. Keep about a quarter on one side and put the rest in a bowl. Cover with cold water, sprinkle with the salt and leave for 30 minutes or so.

Heat 3 tablespoons of the oil in a saucepan. Add the handful of onion and the chopped garlic and sauté until golden. Add the tomato and season lightly with salt and pepper. Cook for 5–10 minutes until the tomato has melted and the water evaporated and you can see the oil actually frying. Remove from the heat and keep aside.

Rinse the lentils and pick out any hard odd bits. Put the lentils in a saucepan and cover with cold water. Bring to the boil over high heat. Drain, then return to the saucepan. Add about 1.5 litres (6 cups) hot water and season with salt. Bring back to the boil, then lower the heat slightly and cook, uncovered, for about 20 minutes. Add the tomato mixture and cook for another 10 minutes or so, until the lentils are soft but not mushy and there is not much liquid left. Stir occasionally to make sure they don't stick to the pan. If it seems like the lentils are drying out, add a little more hot water.

Heat 1 tablespoon of oil in a saucepan and add the whole clove of garlic. Add the rice, season with salt, mix through and cook for a minute. Add enough water to come about 3 cm (about an inch) above the top of the rice and bring to the boil, stirring once. Cook uncovered for 3–4 minutes, until a lot of the water seems to have evaporated and there are some holes on the surface. Drizzle with a tablespoon of oil, cover the pan and lower the heat to a minimum. Cook for about 15 minutes, or until the rice is dry and steaming, then fluff it up with a fork to make sure it hasn't stuck to the pan. Remove from the heat and leave the lid on if you are not eating immediately.

Drain and rinse the soaked onion in a fine sieve. Mix with the lemon juice and chilli and a splash of olive oil and season with salt and a little pepper. Arrange a pile of lentils, a pile of rice, a small pile of onion salad and a dollop of yoghurt on each plate — some people will eat them separately while others like to stir it all together on the plate.

You can add to, change, mix up or use a recipe exactly as it is, but the way you put it on the plate and give it away is yours.

Serves 6

1 TEASPOON GROUND CORIANDER
1 TEASPOON GROUND CUMIN
A PINCH OF NUTMEG
^{1}/2 TEASPOON GROUND CARDAMOM
4 CLOVES
1 BAY LEAF
1 HEAPED TABLESPOON GARAM MASALA
A PINCH OF FRESHLY GROUND BLACK PEPPER
100 ml (3^1/2 fl oz) VEGETABLE OIL
1.25 kg (2 lb 12 oz) BONED AND SKINNED
  CHICKEN THIGHS, *cut into bite-sized pieces*
2 ONIONS, *chopped*
45 g (^{1}/2 cup) DESICCATED COCONUT
70 g (^{1}/2 cup) ROASTED, UNSALTED CASHEW
  NUTS, *cut in half*
250 g (1 cup) PLAIN GREEK YOGHURT

CHICKEN, COCONUT &
CASHEW NUT CURRY

This recipe belongs to my friend Maria. She is a fantastic cook and has a real love for ethnic food.

Heat a large non-stick saucepan over high heat. Add the coriander, cumin, nutmeg, cardamom, cloves, bay leaf, garam masala and black pepper. Stir-fry for about a minute, or until you can really smell the spices. Tip out of the pan onto a plate and set aside.

Heat the oil in the saucepan and brown the chicken with the onions. Add the spice mix and stir until you can smell the perfume, making sure it doesn't stick. Season with salt. Add the coconut and 500 ml (2 cups) water and bring to the boil.

Lower the heat, cover and simmer for about 30 minutes, stirring now and then. Add the cashews and cook for another 10 minutes or so. If it seems like the curry needs more liquid, add a little more hot water. You should have a thick sauce. Stir in the yoghurt, turn the heat down to minimum and simmer for a minute or so, without allowing to boil. Serve with rice with butter and lemon, and the carrot and cardamom salad (pages 356–7).

Serves 4–6

160 ml (²/3 cup) OLIVE OIL
1 CHICKEN (1.3 kg/3 lb), CUT INTO 8 PORTIONS
A SMALL BUNCH OF CORIANDER (CILANTRO)
100 g (3¹/2 oz) ENGLISH SPINACH
2 GARLIC CLOVES, *chopped*
2 CARROTS, *diced*
¹/2 RED PEPPER (CAPSICUM), *seeded and diced*
50 g (¹/3 cup) FRESH *or* FROZEN PEAS
1 TEASPOON CAYENNE PEPPER (OR STRONG PAPRIKA)
500 g (2¹/4 cups) SHORT-GRAIN RICE (BUT NOT
  PUDDING RICE)
CHILLIES IN OIL, (PAGE 160), *to serve*

spiced yoghurt
250 g (1 cup) PLAIN GREEK YOGHURT
1 TEASPOON GROUND CUMIN
2 TEASPOONS OLIVE OIL

CHICKEN
WITH CORIANDER
& SPINACH RICE

This is another of my friend Ana's recipes. It is a little like a Peruvian pilaf. When we made it for the first time in Italy, after just one mouthful her husband had a look on his face as if he had found something. The Peruvians were all nodding and clucking in agreement that there was enough of this and that... there could have been more of this... but that it was just right. Just the way they knew and had grown up with. I added the spiced yoghurt and even Ana thought it was a good addition. Leave out the chilli oil if you are feeding children.

Heat half the olive oil in a large heavy-based pan and fry the chicken until it is browned and crusty on all sides and just about cooked. Remove from the heat and discard the oil from the pan.

Break off the coriander leaves from the stems (freeze the stems for later use) and purée in a small food processor with the spinach and 125 ml (¹/2 cup) water.

Heat the remaining oil in the same pan and add the garlic. When you begin to smell it, add the carrots, pepper and peas. Sauté for 5 minutes to soften, then add the cayenne pepper and mix through. Add the coriander and spinach purée and cook for a couple of minutes before adding the chicken. Season with salt and pepper. Sauté for a minute to mix the flavours and then add 750 ml (3 cups) water. Bring to the boil, then cover, lower the heat to medium and cook for about 15 minutes for the chicken to absorb all the flavours.

Remove the chicken to a plate and add the rice to the pan, together with 500 ml (2 cups) hot water (or enough to cover the rice by about 3 cm/1¼ inches). Cook, uncovered, for 5 or 10 minutes, or until the rice seems to have absorbed most of the water. Lower the heat to an absolute minimum, cover, and cook for about 15 minutes, or until the rice is cooked. Stir only a couple of times during cooking, so that it doesn't stick. Check the seasoning. If you are not serving immediately, cook the rice for a little less time, then turn it off and leave covered for 5 or 10 minutes to steam.

To make the spiced yoghurt, mix together the yoghurt, cumin and olive oil and season with salt and pepper.

Pile the rice on a large serving platter. Arrange the chicken on the rice and each person can add a dollop of spiced yoghurt and a drizzling of chilli oil to their own serving. Serve hot or at room temperature.

Serves 4

4 *or* 5 LARGE POTATOES, *peeled*
2 HEAPED TABLESPOONS GRAINY MUSTARD
JUICE OF 2 LEMONS *(but save the squeezed lemon halves)*
1 TABLESPOON DRIED OREGANO *or* THYME,
   crumbled
4 TABLESPOONS OLIVE OIL
1 MEDIUM-SIZED CHICKEN (about 1.3 kg/3 lb)
2 RED ONIONS, *peeled and cut into wedges*
2 BAY LEAVES
6 GARLIC CLOVES, *with their skin left on*
125 ml (¹/₂ cup) WHITE WINE

LUDI'S
CHICKEN

This is my sister Tanja's recipe. Ludi is a nickname: she calls me Ludi, and I call her Ludi (our children often look puzzled). This dish just seems to work for all ages and however many people happen to end up eating. You can even serve it at room temperature and the potatoes still end up tasting good — which is not a common thing for roast potatoes, really.

Preheat the oven to 180 C (350 F/Gas 4). Halve the potatoes lengthways and then cut them into three or four pieces so that they look like giant chips.

Mix together the mustard, lemon juice, oregano and olive oil to make a marinade. Put the chicken, potatoes, onion wedges, bay leaves and 4 garlic cloves in a large oven dish. Season the potatoes and chicken (outside and in the cavity) with salt and pepper. Put two of the squeezed lemon halves and the remaining garlic in the chicken cavity. Splash the marinade over the chicken and potatoes, shuffling them around with your hands so they are well coated. Gently pour a cupful of water into the dish (trying not to wash away the marinade). Roast for about 1 hour.

After an hour the top of the chicken should be getting brown. Pour the wine over the top, turn the potatoes and onions, and roast for another hour, turning the chicken when it is well browned on top. Check that the potatoes are still in a little liquid — if they look dry, add a little more hot water.

The chicken should be golden brown, juicy and cooked through. If it seems done but you think the potatoes might need longer, remove the chicken to a warmed serving platter. The potatoes, however, should not be crispy but golden and juicy and there should be a little sauce in the dish to serve with the chicken. If it is dry, add some hot water to the dish and scrape the bits from the bottom and sides to make more sauce. Serve hot or even at room temperature.

Bring the lamb to room temperature for about 30 minutes before you want to cook it. Preheat the oven to 200°C (400°F/Gas 6). Line a oven tray with aluminium foil (to make cleaning up easier) and fit it with a rack. Shake the lamb out of the marinade and put it on the rack so the bottom doesn't touch the tray. Cook for about an hour, turning once, until the lamb is deep golden and a firm crust has formed. If, when you turn the lamb over, some of the marinade has come away, then brush on some more. The lamb should be cooked through inside.

Meanwhile, heat half the olive oil in a small saucepan. Gently sauté the spring onions until they are very lightly golden, then add about 3 tablespoons of water and cook for another few minutes until the water has reduced and the onions are soft and dry. Remove from the heat, stir in the ginger and leave to cool. Transfer to a serving bowl and stir in the coriander, lime juice, remaining olive oil and a dash of chillies in oil, then season with salt.

Leave the lamb to stand for at least 10 minutes before carving. Serve with a spoonful of the spring onion, ginger and coriander relish alongside.

We had marimekko bedcovers and sheets, and gorgeous bright colours in our tablecloths and hand-woven floor rugs. We drank mainly from Itaala glasses and ate cooked-for-hours Greek lamb.

Serves 8–10

350 g (12 oz) SUGAR
1 LITRE (4 cups) MILK
1 TEASPOON VANILLA EXTRACT
6 EGGS

CREME
CARAMEL

I have always loved this effortless dessert. It doesn't scream for attention, and its lightness and gentle caramel flavour need no extra decoration.

Preheat the oven to 160°C (310°F/Gas 2). To make the caramel, put 200 g (7 oz) of the sugar and a few drops of water in a heavy-based saucepan over high heat. As soon as the side starts to colour, lower the heat and swirl the pan around to distribute the heat. Watch the sugar closely as it can burn in a second.

When the caramel is deep gold, remove it from the heat and immediately pour it into a 24 cm (9½ inch) cake or ring tin, or into 8 or 10 small ramekins. Holding the tin with a cloth, swirl it around to quickly spread the caramel all over the base and a little up the side. Take care as it sets quickly. Set the tin aside while you make the custard.

Heat the milk in a saucepan until almost boiling, then remove from the heat. Whisk together the vanilla, eggs and the rest of the sugar in a large bowl. Add a ladleful of the hot milk to the eggs to acclimatise them, and whisk to prevent them from cooking. Slowly add the rest of the milk to the eggs, trying not to make them too frothy.

Strain the custard carefully into a large jug and then pour onto the caramel. Put the tin in a deep baking dish and carefully pour enough boiling water into the dish to come halfway up the side of the tin. Bake for 50–60 minutes in the centre of the oven until the top is golden in parts, quite set but still a little wobbly. Remove from the oven and from the water bath, and leave to cool. Cover with plastic wrap and refrigerate for at least a few hours (or overnight) before serving.

Gently loosen the side of the crème caramel with the back of a spoon or your fingers. Put a large serving dish (with a slight rim to contain the caramel juice) upside down over your pudding. Holding the plate and cake tin firmly with your fingers, carefully and quickly flip them over, so that the plate is the right way up and the pudding plops gently down with the caramel sauce. Serve thick slices with the caramel spooned over.

Serves 6

200 ml (7 fl oz) MILK
150 g (5¹/2 oz) SEMI-SWEET DARK CHOCOLATE,
  broken into pieces
1 TEASPOON VANILLA EXTRACT
2 EGGS, *separated*
40 g (1¹/2 oz) CASTER (SUPERFINE) SUGAR
200 ml (7 fl oz) POURING (SINGLE) CREAM

BAKED CHOCOLATE PUDDINGS

These are rich and delicious, yet not too heavy, and I think they are best served straight from the fridge. You will need six individual oven saucepans or ramekins of 150 ml (5 fl oz) capacity.

Preheat the oven to 200°C (400°F/Gas 6). Put the milk and chocolate in a saucepan and heat until completely melted. Stir often so that the chocolate doesn't stick. Add the vanilla.

Whip the egg whites in a small clean bowl until fluffy peaks form. Set them aside (you could put them in the fridge) and work quickly so the whites don't deflate. In a separate bowl, whisk the yolks and sugar until combined. Whisk in a ladleful of the chocolate milk so that the eggs don't scramble, and then add the rest in a slow steady stream, whisking continuously. Whisk in the cream. Fold in the egg whites and spoon into six ovenproof 150 ml (5 fl oz) ramekins.

Sit the ramekins in a deep baking dish. Carefully pour enough boiling water into the dish to come halfway up the side of the ramekins. Bake for 25–30 minutes, or until the puddings are slightly crusty on the surface. Remove from the water bath and leave to cool. Serve warm, or refrigerate and serve cold with cream or a very light dusting of icing (confectioners') sugar.

Serves 8

100 g (3¹/₂ oz) BUTTER, *plus extra for greasing*
100 g (3¹/₂ oz) CASTER (SUPERFINE) SUGAR
100 g (3¹/₂ oz) SEMI-SWEET DARK CHOCOLATE, *broken into pieces*
3 EGGS, *separated*
1 TEASPOON VANILLA EXTRACT
20 g (3/4 oz) CAKE FLOUR *or* PLAIN (ALL-PURPOSE) FLOUR, *plus extra for dusting*
40 g (1¹/₂ oz) FINELY GROUND HAZELNUTS

hot chocolate
375 ml (1¹/₂ cups) POURING (SINGLE) CREAM
100 g (3¹/₂ oz) SEMI-SWEET DARK CHOCOLATE, *broken into pieces*

CHOCOLATE
TRUFFLE TART WITH
HOT CHOCOLATE

Serve this in small portions: it is enough for eight people and is just on the right side of richness in a tiny slice. On its own it is gorgeous with a pile of fresh fruit and another pile of crème fraiche. If you prefer an icing to the little espresso cups of wintery hot chocolate, then melt 150 ml (5 fl oz) of cream with 150 g (5 oz) of chocolate and pour over the cooled cake.

Preheat the oven to 180°C (350°F/Gas 4). Butter and flour a 20 cm (8 inch) springform cake tin. Melt the butter in a small saucepan over low heat. Add the sugar and chocolate and stir until the chocolate melts and the sugar dissolves. Remove from the heat and scrape into a mixing bowl. Leave to cool for about 30 minutes. Add the egg yolks and vanilla and whisk in well with an electric mixer. Sift in the flour and whisk until well combined, then fold in the hazelnuts.

Whip the egg whites until very fluffy and then fold through the chocolate mixture a spoonful at a time. Scrape the mixture into the cake tin and bake for about 35 minutes, or until a skewer inserted comes out clean and the cake feels firm and is a little cracked on the top. Leave to cool for at least 15 minutes or so before you remove it from the tin.

To make the hot chocolate, put the cream in a saucepan and bring to the boil. Add the chocolate, stirring until it is thick and smooth and the chocolate has completely melted. Pour into espresso cups and serve with little wedges of cake.

Serves 10

200 g (7 oz) SEMI-SWEET DARK CHOCOLATE
250 g (9 oz) BUTTER
100 g (3¹/2 oz) CASTER (SUPERFINE) SUGAR
5 EGGS
100 ml (3¹/2 fl oz) BRANDY
150 g (5¹/2 oz) CAKE FLOUR OR PLAIN (ALL-PURPOSE)
   FLOUR
1 TABLESPOON BAKING POWDER

syrup
220 g (1 cup) SUGAR

MOIST
CHOCOLATE
CAKE

This can be served all on its own with a cup of coffee, or more dressed up as a Black-Forest type of dessert with a pile of fresh fruit such as cherries, raspberries or clementines and a dollop of whipped cream or crème fraiche.

Preheat your oven to 180°C (350°F/Gas 4). Butter and flour a 26 cm (10¹/2 inch) cake tin. Melt the chocolate with the butter and sugar in a heatproof bowl set over a saucepan of barely simmering water, making sure that the bowl isn't touching the water. Stir until the chocolate has melted and then remove from the heat to cool a little.

Whip the eggs in a large bowl until they have fluffed up well. Slowly pour in the melted chocolate mixture, whisking until it is all incorporated. Whisk in the brandy. Sift in the flour, baking powder and a pinch of salt and then whisk in well until there are no lumps of flour. Scrape out the mixture into the tin and bake for about 45 minutes, until a skewer inserted into the centre comes out clean and the top is firm and a bit crusty. Remove from the oven and make a few holes in the top with a skewer.

While the cake is baking, make a syrup by boiling the sugar with 300 ml (10¹/2 fl oz) water for about 5 minutes until it has thickened. Set aside to cool. Pour the cooled syrup evenly over the cooled cake (don't miss out the dome of the cake if it is slightly rounded from baking). The cake will absorb the syrup and remain soft and moist. Invert the cake onto a flat plate before serving.

Serves 8–10

1 kg (2 lb 4 oz) BERRIES
200 g (7 oz) CASTER (SUPERFINE) SUGAR
500 g (1 lb 2 oz) DAY-OLD WHITE LOAF
250 ml (1 cup) THICK (DOUBLE/HEAVY) CREAM
2 TABLESPOONS ICING (CONFECTIONERS')
  SUGAR
1 TEASPOON VANILLA EXTRACT
250 g (9 oz) MASCARPONE

SUMMER
PUDDING

You can use one single type of berries — raspberries, blackberries, blackcurrants, redcurrants — depending on what you like and what's in season. If you use frozen berries, leave them out for a while to thaw before you start. I like this with a mascarpone cream, but you could also serve it with crème fraiche, vanilla ice cream or ordinary whipped cream.

Put the berries and caster sugar in a large saucepan with 125 ml (1/2 cup) water and heat gently for 2 minutes. Remove from the heat. Pour off the juice and keep this on one side. (Taste for sweetness and, if you prefer your berries a bit sweeter, add a little more sugar.)

Cut the crusts from the bread and cut the bread horizontally into slices about 1/2 cm (1/4 inch) thick. Dip the bread in the berry juice and then line the base and side of a 2-litre (8-cup) pudding bowl. You can patch here and there with the bread, so there are no spaces anywhere. Leave the bread tops sticking up for now. You should have a few slices of bread left over.

Spoon the berries into the bread-lined bowl and cover with the remaining bread to form a lid (make sure there are no gaps as this will be the bottom of your pudding). Dribble more berry juice over the top so that there is no white bread anywhere to be seen, and trim away any bits of bread that are sticking up. Then find a plate that fits perfectly inside the rim of your bowl and sit it firmly on the bread lid. Find something fairly heavy (like a tin of tomatoes) to put on top of the plate and then refrigerate overnight.

Just before serving, make the mascarpone cream. Whip the cream in a bowl with the icing sugar and vanilla until it just starts to thicken. Whisk in the mascarpone to make a nice thick cream. Turn the pudding out onto a serving plate (if it won't come out easily, dip the base briefly in hot water) and serve in wedges with a dollop of cream. If you have any berry juice left over, drizzle it over the top.

Serves 8

250 g (2 cups) CAKE FLOUR OR PLAIN (ALL-PURPOSE)
   FLOUR, *plus extra for dusting*
120 g (¹/2 cup) SUGAR
2 TEASPOONS BAKING POWDER
120 g (4 oz) BUTTER, *softened, plus extra for greasing*
1 EGG
185 ml (3/4 cup) MILK
1 TEASPOON VANILLA EXTRACT
300 ml (10¹/2 fl oz) THICK (DOUBLE/HEAVY) CREAM
200 g (²/3 cup) HOME-MADE JAM (not too sweet)
ICING (CONFECTIONERS') SUGAR, *to serve*

JAM
& CREAM
SHORTCAKE

This is another cake that my mother makes often. It is delicious, honest and quick and easy to make. It doesn't keep very well once it is filled so, if you won't be serving it immediately, keep the cake covered in plastic wrap once it has cooled and just cut it and spread with the jam and cream before serving. Use any flavour jam you like — just not too sweet. I love this with home-made quince and grape jam. If you don't have any jam, you could use fresh berries.

Preheat the oven to 190°C (375°F/Gas 5). Grease and flour a 24 cm (9¹/2 inch) springform cake tin.

Sift the flour into a bowl with the sugar, baking powder and a pinch of salt. Add the butter and use an electric mixer or wooden spoon to quickly mix it together. Whisk the egg and milk together in a small bowl and add to the batter. Mix in quickly to incorporate it. You should have a soft thick batter.

Pour the batter into the cake tin and bake for about 30 minutes, or until the cake is lightly golden. Remove from the oven and cool slightly, then remove from the cake tin and leave to cool completely.

Slice the cake in half horizontally. Slide the bottom half onto a serving plate. Whisk the vanilla into the cream so that it is quite stiff. Spread the jam over the bottom layer of cake and then carefully spread the cream over the jam. Cover with the top layer of the cake and dust with icing sugar.

Serves 6

600 ml (21 fl oz) MILK
300 ml (10¹/2 fl oz) POURING (SINGLE) CREAM
1 LEVEL TEASPOON GROUND CINNAMON
280 ml (3/4 cup) RUNNY HONEY

MILK,
HONEY & CINNAMON
ICE CREAM

You could use a honey lightly flavoured with lavender or eucalyptus that will show up in the taste of your ice cream, but just a plain runny honey will do. You might like to add a couple of egg yolks to the cream for some extra richness, but I love this wholesome and simple. Your ice cream may not freeze completely firm, depending on your choice of honey — instead it might have a lovely creamy texture.

Put the milk, cream and cinnamon in a saucepan over low heat so that the flavours mingle. Stir in the honey and increase the heat until just coming to the boil. Remove from the heat and leave to cool. Transfer to a bowl, cover and put in the freezer.

After an hour, remove the bowl from the freezer, give an energetic whisk with a hand whisk or electric mixer and return to the freezer. Whisk again after another couple of hours. When it is nearly firm, give one last whisk, transfer to a suitable freezing container with a lid and let it set in the freezer until it is firm (depending on the type of honey you use, your ice cream may not freeze completely solid).

Alternatively, pour the mixture into your ice-cream machine and freeze, following the manufacturer's instructions.

Serves 4

250 ml (1 cup) POURING (SINGLE) CREAM
250 ml (1 cup) MILK
230 g (8 oz) CASTER (SUPERFINE) SUGAR
GRATED RIND OF 1 LEMON
JUICE OF 2 SMALL LEMONS
PULP OF 6 FRESH PASSIONFRUIT

PASSIONFRUIT
ICE CREAM

This is my friend Carl's recipe. He is an excellent cook and likes to serve this with crisp, deep-fried, sugar-dusted pastry ribbons. This is one of my favourite favourites.

Put the cream, milk and sugar in a bowl and stir until dissolved. Cover and put the bowl in the freezer. After an hour, remove the bowl from the freezer and give an energetic whisk with a hand whisk or electric mixer, then return it to the freezer. Whisk again after another couple of hours, this time whisking in the lemon rind, juice and passionfruit pulp. Return it to the freezer. When it is nearly firm, give one last whisk, transfer to a suitable freezing container with a lid and let it set in the freezer until it is firm.

Alternatively, pour the mixture into your ice-cream machine and freeze, following the manufacturer's instructions.

My parents are like perfume and meatballs. In their looks they are equally striking, each clearly representing their own nation.

Serves 4

170 g (3/4 cup) CASTER (SUPERFINE) SUGAR
500 ml (2 cups) WARM MILK
250 ml (1 cup) POURING (SINGLE) CREAM
4 EGG YOLKS

CARAMEL
ICE CREAM

This is a beautiful, buttery toffee-brown that looks wonderful sitting alongside a scoop of banana sorbet. Serve it with some dark chocolate sticks for a rich and complete dessert.

Put the sugar in a saucepan over medium heat and let it melt slowly and turn to caramel. Don't stir the sugar, just tilt the pan occasionally so that it melts evenly and turns a deep gold. Slowly and very carefully add the warm milk, standing back as it will splash up. Add the cream and mix through well.

Whip the egg yolks with electric beaters until they are fluffy. Add a ladleful of the caramel mixture, whisking constantly so that you don't scramble the eggs. Gradually add the rest of the caramel mixture. Return the whole lot to a saucepan over very low heat and cook, stirring constantly with a wooden spoon, until the mixture thickens slightly.

Remove from the heat and leave to cool, stirring from time to time. When completely cool, transfer to a bowl, cover and put in the freezer.

After an hour, remove the bowl from the freezer, give an energetic whisk with a hand whisk or electric mixer and return to the freezer. Whisk again after another couple of hours. When it is nearly firm, give one last whisk, transfer to a suitable container with a lid and let it set in the freezer until it is solid.

Alternatively, pour the mixture into your ice-cream machine and freeze, following the manufacturer's instructions.

Serves 4

60 g (2¹/₄ oz) BUTTER
200 g (7 oz) CASTER (SUPERFINE) SUGAR
375 ml (1¹/₂ cups) POURING (SINGLE) CREAM, plus 1 tablespoon
2 JUICY PEARS (about 450 g/1 lb), *peeled, quartered and cored*
125 ml (¹/₂ cup) MILK
1 TEASPOON VANILLA EXTRACT

PEAR
CARAMEL
ICE CREAM

I love fruit caramel ice creams. You can try this with apples, plums,
peaches and maybe bananas. Serve with a buttery shortbread-type biscuit.

Put the butter and sugar in a saucepan over medium heat for about 10 minutes, until liquid and
caramelised. Carefully add the 1 tablespoon of cream and simmer for a minute before adding
the pear quarters. Turn them around in the caramel and simmer for 5 minutes. Lift out the
pears with a slotted spoon, allowing any caramel to drip back into the pan. Purée the pears in a
blender and set aside.

Put the cream, milk and vanilla in a bowl and whip for a few minutes until the mixture
thickens and you notice an increase in volume. Whisk in the puréed pears and 125 ml (¹/₂ cup)
of the slightly cooled caramel (save the rest for later). Cover the bowl and put in the freezer.

After an hour, remove the bowl from the freezer, give an energetic whisk with a hand whisk or
electric mixer and return to the freezer. Whisk again after another couple of hours. When it is
nearly firm, give one last whisk, swirl in the remaining caramel and make a few loops through
the ice cream with a spoon. Transfer to a suitable freezing container with a lid and let it set in
the freezer until it is firm.

Alternatively, pour the mixture into your ice-cream machine and freeze, following the
manufacturer's instructions. Remove the ice cream from the freezer 5 or 10 minutes before
serving to let it soften a little.

There are some things that don't change much. I find the smell of a dish, or the way a certain spice is crushed, or just a quick look at the way something has been put on a plate, can pull me back to another place and time. I love those memories that seem so far away, yet you can hold them and carry them with you, even forget them, and then, with a single taste or hint of a smell, be chaperoned back to a beautiful moment.

Index

from Tessa...

This is my chance to thank all of you who, knowingly or unknowingly, helped me to make this book by showering me with inspiration, courage and recipes. To Giovanni and my mice, Yasmine and Cassia, for always filling me with new hope and ideas. To George, Sipi, Tanja and Nicholas for their unwavering support and friendship. To my perfect Italian 'grandparent' cooks (the type that I always search for along my trails), Mario and Wilma Neri, who still amaze me with their readiness to help, no matter what nationality is cooking.

Thank you to dear Kay and everyone at Murdoch for their encouragement and trust: Katy for her courage on her mammoth task; Diana and Jane for their enthusiasm to dance; and Amanda and Juliet, just for saying 'yes'.

Thank you all: Anette, Evelyn, Ana, Artemis, Niki, Maria, Adam, Jem, Stephen, Carl, Jason, Allan and his mum Sue, Silvana, Herve, Ritva Dahl, Ritva Tunaainen, Harriet, Iria, Vania, Yiota, Jenny, Stamos, Natasha, Julia, Fabio, Massimiliano, Mikela, Julietta and Aureliano, Giacomo and Angela, Luisa and Luca, Marco and Lorella, Massimo, Sergio, Beppe, Toni, Daniele, Franco, Andrea and Barbara, Nicci and Brenda, Serena, Gianluca, Bernard and Lisa's gran.

To my always-inspiration: Angela Dwyer, Albert Clarke, Corinne Young, Liz Benatar, Ketty Koufonicola-Touros, Jo Capell and Vivian.

And a big, big acknowledgement to Michail Touros, Manos Chatzikonstantis and Lisa Greenberg for skipping all the way with me.